Nonprofit Finance for Hard Times

Nonprofit Finance for Hard Times

Leadership Strategies When Economies Falter

SUSAN U. RAYMOND, Ph.D.

**With Contributions by
Michael P. Hoffman**

John Wiley & Sons, Inc.

Published by John Wiley & Sons, Inc., Hoboken, New Jersey.
Published simultaneously in Canada.

For general information on our other products and services or for technical support, please contact our Customer Care Department within the United States at (800) 762-2974, outside the United States at (317) 572-3993 or fax (317) 572-4002.

Wiley also publishes its books in a variety of electronic formats. Some content that appears in print may not be available in electronic books. For more information about Wiley products, visit our web site at www.wiley.com.

Library of Congress Cataloging-in-Publication Data:

Raymond, Susan Ueber.
  Nonprofit finance for hard times : leadership strategies when economies falter / Susan U. Raymond.
    p. cm.
  Includes index.
  ISBN 978-0-470-49010-5 (cloth)
  1. Nonprofit organizations—Finance. 2. Nonprofit organization—Management.
  3. Fund raising. I. Title.

HG4027.65.R396 2009   2009031704
658.15–dc22

Printed in the United States of America
10 9 8 7 6 5 4 3 2 1

For colleagues, here and abroad,
who have encouraged this work.
With friends, everything is possible.
Without them, all is lost.

Contents

List of Exhibits

List of Cases and Commentary

Preface

The two most important considerations for any organization faced with scarce resources are efficiency of operations and effectiveness of effort. This is (or ought to be) as true in the nonprofit as it is in the commercial sector. As this book vividly points out, however, the past decades of change and growth among American nonprofits has created a serious problem for the sector.

On the one hand, the strength of nonprofit and philanthropic activity is its breadth. The nation's 1.2 million nonprofits address an extraordinary sweep of societal needs, from storefront clinics to cancer research, from the air quality of a small town to the astrophysics of the universe. Nothing is too small, and few things are too large, for the efforts of nonprofits.

On the other hand, that very strength is itself an emerging weakness. Proliferation of organizations has led to duplication, replication, and fears of inefficiency. The growth of philanthropy has not kept pace, and many (perhaps most) nonprofits find increasing competition for resources. In an economic crisis, such as that of 2008–2009, severe resource constraints make the social price of inefficiency exceedingly high.

What is needed is entrepreneurial innovation in the way we are organized and in the way we work. Philanthropies and nonprofits must seek ways to cut through duplication and find collaborative synergies. The emphasis must be on demonstrated effectiveness and efficiency. That demonstration, in turn, will trigger an outpouring of even more philanthropy as people come to trust that every dollar is being put to work to its highest value for the purpose of solving problems.

It is a challenge to constantly emphasize maximum value of the investment dollar in the commercial sector. It is even more of a challenge in the nonprofit sector where clear measures of alternative social returns to the use of a philanthropic dollar are often not clear and are usually not shared among competing organizations. But always, and even more in times of economic difficulty, when demands are great and resources are limited, that hard job must be undertaken with dedicated diligence.

Nonprofit Finance for Hard Times documents the evolution of nonprofit and philanthropic institutions in the United States. It emphasizes that preparing for economic difficulties is not a task to be undertaken in crisis; it is a constant responsibility that flows from the core purpose of nonprofits to address our common needs. *Nonprofit Finance for Hard Times* teaches that constant attention to value, constant engagement of community, and constant reexamination of effectiveness is the only pathway to sustainability. It is also the only way to keep faith with those who lend not just wealth, but their most precious commodity—time—to the betterment of our communities and our nation.

William I. Campbell
Senior Advisor
JPMorgan Chase

Acknowledgments

The author would like to thank the following individuals for their assistance in developing this book:

> Josh Moore, Senior Director at Changing Our World, Inc., for assistance with research and management of all illustrations, and for his generosity in reacting to the general concepts contained in this work.
> Mary Beth Martin, Senior Managing Director at Changing Our World, Inc., for review and comment of the analytic framework that underpins the strategy discussion in the final chapters.
> Kathleen Sullivan, President of Operations, and Raissa Smorol, Managing Director, of Changing Our World, Inc., for their review and valuable comments on early drafts.

And, of course, deepest thanks to Mike Hoffman for his contributions to this volume, and for his lifelong leadership in the philanthropic and nonprofit sectors of this country and the world.

About the Author

Susan U. Raymond, Ph.D., is Executive Vice President for Research, Evaluation, and Strategic Planning for Changing Our World, Inc. She has been the Director of Policy Programs and the Director of Strategic Planning and Special Projects at the New York Academy of Sciences, a special advisor to the U.S. Agency for International Development, and a projects officer at the World Bank. Dr. Raymond is also Chief Analyst for onPhilanthropy.com and a member of the Advisory Board of the Institute for Global Prosperity, which publishes the annual *Index on Global Philanthropy*. Dr. Raymond has developed and worked on nonprofit and private foundation development across the United States and in Eastern Europe, the Middle East, and Asia. She earned her BA Phi Beta Kappa from Macalester College and her MA and Ph.D. from the Johns Hopkins University School of Advanced International Studies. Her previous books published by John Wiley & Sons are *Mapping the New World of American Philanthropy: Causes and Consequences of the Transfer of Wealth*, published in 2007, and *The Future of Philanthropy: Economics, Ethics, and Management*, published in 2004.

Nonprofit Finance for Hard Times

CHAPTER 1

Beginning at the Beginning
Public Charities on the Economic Landscape

[Americans] have all the lively faith in the perfectability of man, they judge that the diffusion of knowledge must necessarily be advantageous, and the consequences of ignorance fatal; they all consider society as a body in a state of improvement, humanity as a changing scene, in which nothing is, or ought to be, permanent; and they admit that what appears to them today to be good may be superseded by something better tomorrow.

Alexis de Tocqueville, 1835

Americans have long believed in the ability to perfect society, to solve problems by force of effort. Further, and despite enshrining individualism at the core of its psyche, Americans really do prefer to solve problems together rather than alone. There is a legendary mystique about the dust-covered lone sheriff who rides into town at sunset to rescue the community from the vile hands of evildoers. Legends make excellent movies; they just don't jibe with reality.

Citizen engagement, which is a recurring theme throughout this book, is the more common historical model of community problem solving. The lone voice in the wilderness is less a national role model than the "everyone-in-it-together" potluck dinner fund-raiser for social change.

Thematic Summary

Common, voluntary action on the societal commons has a long history in the United States. But the size and nature of the "nonprofit sector"

(Continued)

(*Continued*)
has changed markedly in the last two decades. Public charities are now a social and an economic force, and financial health and welfare is equally a social and an economic concern when economic turbulence threatens the underpinnings of all institutions.

The nation does not take well to fatalism; it believes betterment is constantly possible.

The exemption from taxation of money or property devoted to charitable or other purposes is based upon the theory that government is compensated for the loss of revenue by its relief from financial burden which would otherwise have to be met by appropriations from public funds, and by the benefits resulting from the promotion of the general welfare.

House Ways and Means Committee Report to Congress, 1939

The role of public charities on the societal commons to pursue that betterment is as old as the nation itself. Private effort through charitable institutions to address community social needs had its roots in religious organizations, but the branches and leaves quickly grew in multiple directions and gave rise to nonreligious groupings of like-minded individuals focused on mutual aid. That early growth was not motivated by tax benefits. Formal tax-exempt status for nonprofit charities is relatively recent, beginning with the 1913 Revenue Act, which imposed federal corporate income taxes for the first time but explicitly exempted charities. Still, the legal roots of the concept of some type of tax relief for charities are older. The Tariff Act of 1894 and the Revenue Act of 1909 both contained foreshadowing of the 1913 initiative, indicating a long-standing concern among lawmakers that formal organizations established for the public good be treated differently from those organized for private gain.[1] The intent—at least in part—was to encourage private investment in meeting societal needs in order to avoid the public budget costs of equivalent government action. If private voluntary action could forestall tax expenditures, then the culture of U.S. governance could opt for the former over the latter.

The Present Departs from the Past

All was quiet for about 40 years. By the 1950s, however, concerns were growing that large nonprofits were engaging in activities akin to private commerce, and lawmakers began to take a closer look at the evolving collision course between tax exemption and the marketplace. Tax exemption was feared to be a veil behind which nonprofit organizations obtained market advantage, which they would then use for their own institutional interests quite apart from social needs. Despite *sotto voce* murmurings from commercial institutions and in the halls of Congress, there was no great public outcry, and policy concerns remained nascent. That was, in part, because the problem was largely invisible. According to testimony of the Internal Revenue Service to Congress in 1953, there were only 32,000 public charities in the United States, a number too small to be the focus of anyone's statistical attention.[2]

That was about to change, and change radically, in two ways. First, in midcentury, most secular nonprofits were not public charities. They were fraternal organizations, civic societies, and the like, so their numbers were small and engagement with service to members was large, but their interface with the larger public was small. Indeed, by the late 1960s only 32 percent of nonprofits were 501(c)(3) public charities. As recently as the early 1990s, that portion had risen to only 50 percent. As can be seen in Exhibit 1.1, however, the period of the last 16 years has seen an explosion of growth in the number of public charities and a shift in proportions. Now there are some 1.2 million public charities in the nation, a quadrupling in the last 25 years, and they represent nearly two-thirds of all registered nonprofits. Public charities are no longer invisible.

The second related change is the consequent economic role. Rather than simply the recipients of public largess, nonprofits are increasingly a

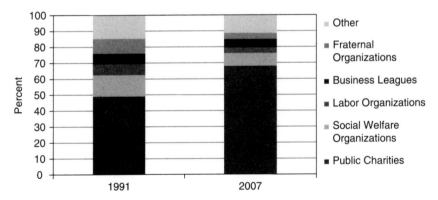

EXHIBIT 1.1 Change in Distribution of IRS Section (c) Organizations by Type, 1991–2007
Source: IRS.

powerful force in the economy. Before embarking on an examination of their economic roles, the structure of their revenue, and their health in trying economic times, however, three caveats are in order.

A Complex and Poorly Documented Sector

First, the term "nonprofit sector" covers myriad types of organizations, from soup kitchens to cemeteries to the pension funds of unions and certain types of insurance companies. There are actually more than 25 IRS codes for nonprofit organizations, with varying implications for the tax treatment of their revenues and the monies they either make or that are donated to them. Exhibit 1.2 illustrates the relative size of each of the categories based on registrations with the Internal Revenue Service.[3]

For purposes of this book, the term "nonprofit" refers only to public charities that are categorized under section 501(c)(3) of the Internal Revenue Service tax code. This represents the nearly two-thirds of all nonprofits and 69 percent of the revenue in the total sector.[4] If only the median rate of growth of the last two decades holds (that is, growth every year is at the middle point of growth rates that have already been seen) there will be 1.7 million public charities by 2015.[5] Exhibit 1.3 depicts this growth. Extraordinary growth, in turn, means extraordinary youthfulness in the sector. Astonishingly, nearly three-quarters of those charities were created since 1980. Parenthetically, this robust growth has not been seen in other types

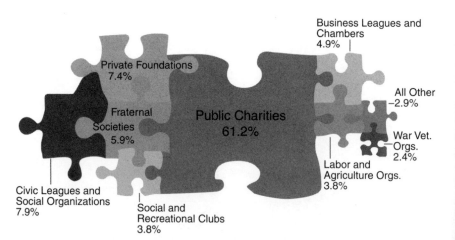

EXHIBIT 1.2 Distribution of All Types of Nonprofits

Source: IRS.

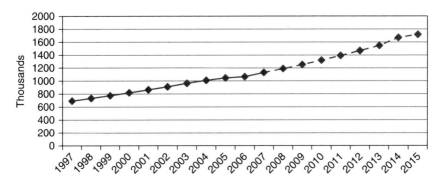

EXHIBIT 1.3 Number of Nonprofits, 1997 Projected to 2015
Source: 1997–2007 IRS; 2007–2015 author projection.

of nonprofits. The number of fraternal organizations, which dominated the sector in the mid-twentieth century, has declined by a third since 1991. So the proliferation has not been driven by some universal increase in the propensity to reject profit in preference to nonprofit among those who form organizations. Rather, growth seems driven by a combination of mission on the societal commons, and possibly, as is discussed in Chapter 3, "Philanthropy within Financial Structure," increasing government reliance on private institutions for community problem solving.

It is important to be sure that terms are correctly and consistently used. A 501(c)(3) public charity is one that is organized and operated exclusively for religious, charitable, scientific, public safety, literary, educational, or amateur sports competition purpose; does not distribute net earnings to the benefit of private shareholders or individuals; and does not, as a substantial part of its activities, seek to influence legislation or participate in political campaigns.[6] A 501(c)(3) does not pay taxes on its net balance at the end of the year (although, as noted later, it must pay taxes on unrelated business income), and donations to it by individuals and organizations are deductible from income for purposes of the donors' income tax calculation.

Narrowing the topic to this subset of "nonprofits" helps little, however. The universe of public charities is itself exceedingly wide. It encompasses huge institutions, such as Harvard University and the Memorial Sloan Kettering Cancer Center, with hundreds of millions of dollars in income and billions of dollars of endowment funds; and small institutions, such as halfway houses and storefront clinics with only tens of thousands of dollars of income and no endowments at all. Nonprofits are half of the nation's hospitals, a third of its health-care clinics, 80 percent of its family and children's centers, and nearly half of its universities.[7] Generalizations about the public charity subsector of the nonprofit sector are, therefore, difficult.

Where possible and when necessary, this work will qualify its analysis by controlling for organizational size.

The data on nonprofit finance are imperfect at best. There is irony here. As noted below, nonprofit organizations represent the third-largest segment of the U.S. economy after the wholesale and the retail trade. Little is known with any precision that reflects the traditions of charity in the country. The historic policy and public attitude has been that organizations selflessly serving the public good should not be held to overly rigid reporting standards. The assumption appears to have been that because these institutions were largely supported by private voluntary contributions and volunteer labor, burdensome financial reporting was, at a minimum, unnecessary. Indeed, demanding rigorous reporting standards could even be seen as something of a violation of the compact of public trust between the people and those institutions that addressed societal ills.

The problem with the data is made even more complex because tax exempt public charities that are part of religious institutions do not need to report to the IRS at all. So we do not know how many religiously affiliated public charities there are, the scope of their operations, or their financial size or structure. Yet a third of private giving flows to religious institutions.[8]

In addition, estimates of giving are based on tax reporting. Individuals may contribute goods, services, and cash to public charities without bothering to include itemized tax forms. The dollar dropped into the firefighter's boot at the corner of Main and Elm, the value of the six-foot hoagie donated to the little league team after a hard-fought championship game, the dollar value of volunteer time—such contributions to the public good through public charitable nonprofits are not captured in official data sets.

Finally, new mechanisms of giving, for example, cause-related marketing (CRM), do not come from philanthropies or philanthropic resources at all. Rather, these revenue streams originate in other budgets, in the case of CRM, in corporate marketing budgets. The dollar value of these new "public good" strategies is not found in any data set, and their presence on the societal commons is often not part of financial estimates in the nonprofit sector at all.

It is important to note that improvements are just over the horizon. Starting in 2009, the Internal Revenue Service will require nonprofits, including small nonprofits, to file their returns on a revised Form 990. The new reporting form asks for more financial and management detail than the previous form. For example, elected officials attending or honored at events must be declared, speaking honoraria revealed, and linkages between these officials and activities or individuals in the nonprofit disclosed. These detailed data will not be available for several years and will not allow comparability to past years for purposes of trend analysis. Still, going forward, the ability to understand the financial structure of tax exempt organizations will be greatly enhanced within five years.

So the data sets used in this work are flawed and can only sketch the outlines of the financial dimensions and structure of the sector. The data sets provide an order-of-magnitude sense of their relationship to the economy, which, in the end, likely understates the importance of the sector overall.

An Economic Engine

Nonprofits represent $1.1 trillion in annual economic spending, the third-largest portion of the economy after the wholesale and the retail trades.[9] Nonprofits of all types represent about 10 percent of national employment, a portion that rises to 17.6 percent in the District of Columbia, 16.5 percent in Vermont, and even 15.6 percent in New York.[10] Indeed, through 2006, nonprofit employment grew faster than overall employment in 46 of the 50 states.[11]

Although no comprehensive data are available nationally, a number of states and communities have examined the full economic effect of their public charitable sectors. Most of this work focuses on education and health care because these service areas represent the largest nonprofit institutions in terms of employment, revenue, and assets.

Several examples suffice to illustrate the degree to which public charities are no longer simply recipients of donations for the poor and needy. They are important sources of jobs, investment, goods, and services.

The arts in the United States generate an estimated $134 billion in economic activity each year, supporting 4.9 million jobs, of which only 2 million are the artists.[12] The Sundance Film Festival produces $60 million in annual revenue for Park City, Utah, fueling jobs throughout the local economy.[13] Hospitals represent a quarter of a trillion dollars in annual wages in the U.S. economy, with rates of increase more than double those in the economy overall.[14] Colleges and universities play a similar outsized economic role. Every campus job is estimated to create 1.6 jobs in the surrounding community, and every dollar spent by an institution of higher education is estimated to generate $1.38 of additional expenditures.[15]

The economic role is not just one of spending and jobs, however. In 2007—admittedly before the market crisis of 2008–2009—the 785 U.S. universities regularly sampled by the *Chronicle of Higher Education* had endowments valued at $411 billion.[16] Between 1995 and 2005, the total assets of public charities rose from $843 billion to $1.98 trillion, an inflation adjusted increase of 84 percent. The assets of public charities represent two-thirds of the assets of all types of nonprofits combined.[17] The nonprofit sector is not just a spender of money; it is an aggregator of capital.

Thus, the health of the nonprofit sector is important to the health of the overall economy. And the health of the economy impacts nonprofits in more ways than simply in the level of the contributions they receive from private citizens and philanthropists. Nonprofits as economic entities must develop revenue strategies for economic decline that integrate philanthropy and fund-raising into broader strategies.

Nonprofits as Masters of Their Own Fate in Economic Turmoil

The charitable sector in the United States has grown from its original roots as a matter of religious commitment to the poor to an $800 billion economic engine. The following chapters examine the role of public charities in the economy, the structure of the revenues and assets that undergirds their operations, and the fate of public charities when the economy, national and local, falls on its regular cyclical hard times.

When economic crisis hits—as it has with a vengeance in the 2008–2009 recessionary period—there is much concern for the health of the nation's nonprofits. That concern is warranted because the nonprofit sector continues to provide much of the safety net for the disadvantaged. But to see nonprofits as simply passive victims is a misperception. Public charities are not victims of economics. They are part of the nation's economic structure. They are (or ought to be) masters of their own destiny, vibrant economic actors with a wide range of revenue options and strategies. Even with robust plans and clear preparation, nonprofits, as economic actors, will not necessarily suffer less than other parts of a stressed economy. But they need not suffer more.

The structure of this book traces the arc of change and its implications for nonprofit revenue in several parts.

Chapter 2 places the discussion of revenue in context. Although the discussion is about revenue, and thus about money, it is important to understand that philanthropy, and the nonprofits it supports, are not simply about money. The sector is a critical anchor of civil society, and the philosophy that underpins that role is critical to keep in the forefront of thought, even as attention turns to money.

Chapters 3 through 5 address the changes in the structure and expectations of the nonprofit and philanthropic sector over the last two decades. These changes provide the environment within which revenue strategy can be developed. The emphasis in these chapters is on rising complexity in the sector, but, more important, with the opportunity that comes with complexity.

Chapter 6 then addresses the economy itself and its relationship with the nonprofit sector. Cycles are actually beneficial to economies, and therefore are to be expected. The relationships to nonprofits and philanthropy are not clear cut, but general trends can be anticipated. Therefore, forward-looking strategy is possible.

Chapter 7 sets out an analytic framework for conceptualizing strategy. Complexity requires some mechanism for arraying options and then aligning them with capacity and the prioritization of choices. The analytic framework provides this tool.

Chapters 8 through 10 address financial strategies for coping with or recovering from economic hard times.

Chapter 11 provides a concluding thought about the imperative of taking on these difficult strategy tasks in the context of civil society.

Chapter 12 contains the commencement address of Michael P. Hoffman to the 2009 graduating class of Malloy College, an address that underscores many of the themes in this book.

Notes

1. P. Arnsberger et al. "A History of the Tax Exempt Sector." *Statistics of Income Bulletin*, (Winter 2008).

2. U.S. House of Representatives, 82nd Congress, 2nd session, 1953. "Hearings before the Select Committee to Investigate Foundations and Comparable Organizations." U.S. Government Printing Office, 64.

3. U.S. Internal Revenue Service, Business Master Files, Exempt Organizations, various years from raw data.

4. A. Blackwood, K. T. Wing, and T. H. Pollak. *The Nonprofit Sector in Brief, 2008*. (Washington, DC: Urban Institute National Center for Charitable Statistics, 2008), 2.

5. Of course, this does not correct for actual operations. Nonprofits register when they are created. There is no mechanism for constantly monitoring their actual operational scope. That a nonprofit exists at a point in time does not mean that it is actually operational at some subsequent point in time.

6. Publication 557, Internal Revenue Service, June 2008.

7. L. M. Salamon and S. L. Geller. "Communique No. 11: Nonprofit Policy Priorities for the New Administration." Johns Hopkins University Center for Civil Society Studies, Listening Post Project, December 2008.

8. *Giving USA*, 2008. Glenville, IL: Giving USA Foundation, 2008.

9. Blackwood et al 2008., op cit.

10. L. M. Salamon and S. W. Sokolowshi. "Employment in America's Charities: A Profile." *Nonprofit Employment Bulletin* 26, Johns Hopkins Center for Civil Society Studies, 2006, 6.

11. State Nonprofit Economic Data Bulletins (various states) from the Nonprofit Employment Data Project, The Johns Hopkins University Center for Civil Society Studies.

12. "Arts and Economic Prosperity." *Americans for the Arts* (2002), www.Americans ForTheArts.org.

13. R. Pogrebin. "Saving Federal Arts Funds: Selling Culture as an Economic Force." *New York Times*, February 16, 2009. C1.

14. S. Raymond. *Non-Profit Hospitals in America: Lives, Jobs and Philanthropy* (New York: Changing Our World, Inc., 2007), 43.

15. S. Raymond. *Enabling the Progress of the Mind: The Future of Philanthropy and Higher Education in America* (New York: Changing Our World, Inc. 2008), 62.

16. Ibid., 66.

17. Blackwood et al., op cit.

CHAPTER 2

Setting the Larger Stage
A Philosophy of Philanthropy

Nor was civil society founded merely to preserve the lives of its members; but that they might live well: for otherwise a state might be composed of slaves, or the animal creation ... nor is it an alliance mutually to defend each other from injuries, or for a commercial intercourse. But whosoever endeavors to establish wholesome laws in a state, attends to the virtues and vices of each individual who composes it; from whence it is evident, that the first care of him who would found a city, truly deserving that name, and not nominally so, must be to have his citizens virtuous.

Aristotle 384 BC–322 BC

The focus of this book is on the revenue implications of—and nonprofit strategies to counteract—economic downturns. Because it is about revenue, the book positions philanthropy as being primarily about money. This is regrettable. "Money" is not only an excessively narrow definition of philanthropy; it dangerously misrepresents the actual role of philanthropy in a civil society. Therefore, before embarking on a detailed assessment of the monetary dimensions of philanthropic strategy in nonprofits constrained by economic crisis, it is important to embed that discussion within a broader philosophy of philanthropy itself. This larger context is not to deny the importance of the monetary dimensions of philanthropy—one does not pay the rent with philosophy, after all—but rather to ensure that those monetary dimensions do not overshadow the broader role of philanthropy in society. The money associated with philanthropy only has meaning in this larger context.

Thematic Summary

It is commitment to community that is the critical characteristic of philanthropy, not the money that changes hands. Dollars themselves are only a shadow of a deeper reality. Where individual passion and leadership flow in a civil society, engagement will follow. And where engagement is to be found, philanthropy will flower.

A Fundamental Question

Let us begin by asking a fundamental question whose response sets the foundation for the author's philosophy of philanthropy: What is the central characteristic of the nonprofit/philanthropic sector that distinguishes it from the commercial sector? The answer is not money. Money is common to both. The answer is not mission. All manner of commercial organizations have missions and are proud to say so on their Web sites and in their showrooms. Indeed, mission as written in the tax code no longer provides guidance. There are many, many for-profit organizations dedicated to education, for example, side by side with nonprofits. The answer is not products and services for which users pay money—more money flows to nonprofits in payment for goods and services than in donations. Nor is it (necessarily) a balance sheet poised on a financial knife's edge. Many nonprofits have healthy fund balances, and many large nonprofits have endowments that are valued in the billions of dollars. In contrast, many commercial institutions (an increasing number in an economy in crisis) fail for lack of funds. Money in the bank—or lack thereof—is not a distinguishing characteristic that allows us to sort the nonprofit from the commercial sector. So what is it that does (or ought to) distinguish the nonprofit/philanthropic sector?

It is one single but complex concept—engagement. The purpose of the sector, and of philanthropy, is to engage private individuals in voluntary action to promote the common good. Everything else—money, products, services, capital—is the means to that end, and only the means. The purpose is voluntary engagement in an open civil society that is the differentiator. Philanthropy that funds nonprofits, and nonprofits themselves, are mechanisms for engaging community—around the corner or around the globe—in dedication to common problem solving. It is a purpose to engage the people in their communities that differentiates, not as a by-product of organizational purpose, but as the purpose itself.

This point must be clarified. As we will see in later chapters, commercial activity, that is, activity that is fundamentally governed by a market, is blending into the societal commons. Renewable energy, for example, clearly serves social needs and does so within enormous markets. Similarly, corporate social responsibility programs that align corporate commercial interest with social good become hybrids of commercial and societal interests. The future will see more of these hybrids and greater permutations and combinations of the for-profit and nonprofit organizational form. The issue is not form; the issue is function. If engagement of the people in common problem solving is the fundamental purpose (not the tactical by-product) of action, then that function extends beyond the commercial into tacit partnership with the nonprofit sector.

Engagement as Differentiator

Now, let us return to philanthropy as money and engagement as the differentiator. Philanthropy—the voluntary transfer of resources to nonprofit organizations and individuals in support of common purposes—is a symbol of individual commitment to common societal cause. It is the commitment to community that is the critical characteristic of philanthropy, not the money that changes hands. Why is this so?

Civil society is the fundamental playing field on which philanthropy takes place and thrives. The London School of Economics defines "civil society" as the arena of uncoerced action around shared interests, purposes, and values, distinct from the state, family, and commerce. Civil society is a form of societal organization that brings individual voluntary action to the societal commons.

Research consistently shows that individuals give to nonprofits when they volunteer. Households that volunteer make annual philanthropic contributions with twice the monetary value of those from households that do not volunteer.[1] Money flows when individuals invest the most valuable resource they have—time—in societal needs, problems, or opportunities. Philanthropy is often a monetary expression of personal commitment to community.

Without personal, voluntary commitment, philanthropy—the monetization of that commitment—will not flow. No one can force anyone to be philanthropic. There is no penalty for the failure to be philanthropic. Even for those who link philanthropic giving to religious obligation, religious belief itself is voluntary at the individual level. Hence, the prerequisite concept for philanthropy is voluntary action of individuals, not in individual self-interest but in the interest of the collective whole.

Discussion of philanthropy as revenue—as money—in this book must not lose sight of the fact that money is a mere shadow of the larger concept of voluntarism in civil society of which philanthropy is an embodiment. One can volunteer and not donate, of course. There is no necessity for monetary philanthropy even where there is robust voluntarism. What elements propel individual voluntarism down the pathway of monetary commitment?

Passion and Leadership

Philanthropy is not simply money. It reflects a passion for community. The most robust, the most sustainable philanthropy comes where the commitment to issues and to community is deepest. That community might be a neighborhood or a nation, down the block or across oceans. The individual who identifies deeply with another group of individuals, who has a passion for the well-being and progress of that community (its human condition, its physical space, its societal peace, its environmental health—whatever might be the measure of "well-being"), is the most reliable philanthropist. Not because of wealth. Not because of possessions. Not because of stature. But because of passion.

The second element that matures volunteerism to philanthropy is leadership. A leader is a person who influences others. It is common to think of "leadership" in philanthropy as being coterminous with size. The megadonor is a leader. The board member is a leader. Anyone who can afford the ticket to the black-tie gala is a leader. The rest? Supporters, donors, "friends of," or a thousand other categories, but certainly not, in the conventional wisdom, leaders.

This is a misrepresentation. Let us return to our definition. A leader is a person who influences others. There is an argument to be made that there is more leadership—greater exemplary power to influence others—on the societal commons from those who give much from little than from those who give little from much. This is so because a greater number of individuals have limited means than have limitless means. The example of a person whom many people consider to be a peer can be more powerful than the example of a person to whom few can relate.

People who donate hard-earned, scarce funds—funds for which there are always alternative uses—do so because they wish to make a difference. By definition, those who engage in philanthropy engage in leadership. They break with individual, insular self-interest and allocate personal earned resources to the commons. In effect, those who give step forward on the societal commons, irrespective of the absolute size of the gift. That gift is a symbol of a deeper willingness to commit to community.

Harnessing these two engines—passion and leadership—lead to concerted and sustainable engagement of individuals on the societal commons. This engagement is the measure of philanthropy's health in our civil society, not the dollars that consequently flow. The root of giving is individual

---

A Public Health "Best Buy": Neglected Tropical Disease Control

Founded in 2006 at the Clinton Global Initiative, the Global Network for Neglected Tropical Diseases (NTDs) is inviting philanthropists at all levels to join in its life-saving work and represents an illustration of how philanthropy can provide an opportunity for all people to make a difference in solving a societal problem.

The Global Network is a first-of-its-kind alliance of international organizations committed to ending global suffering and death from NTDs, a group of 13 parasitic and bacterial infections that thrive in impoverished communities around the world. These diseases affect more than 1.4 billion people around the world and are the most common afflictions of the world's poorest people, most of whom live on less than $1.25 per day.

In January 2009, with an initial investment of $34 million from the Bill & Melinda Gates Foundation, the Global Network launched *End the Neglect 2020*—an international campaign to raise awareness and support to control and eliminate the most debilitating, disfiguring, and deadly NTDs by 2020. This includes delivery of a rapid impact package of four drugs, which are available at low and no cost and which can wipe out seven of the most common NTDs. Delivery of these drugs costs less than 50 cents per person per year, making the effort "a best buy in public health."

Because ending the neglect will require both money and attention, the Global Network is working to educate and involve the public in the impact 50 cents can make. For as much as a newspaper or a pack of gum, donors can make an impact. The campaign also includes the "Loose Change Initiative" as a mechanism to engage grassroots activists in their work, collecting pennies, nickels, dimes, and quarters on campuses, workplaces, and in communities.

Kari Stoever
Managing Director
The Global Network for Neglected Tropical Diseases

---

engagement of the people in their communities. The Founding Fathers understood this deeply. Thomas Jefferson once remarked, "I know of no safe depository of the ultimate powers of the society but the people themselves; and if we think them not enlightened enough to exercise their control with a wholesome discretion, the remedy is not to take it from them, but inform their discretion." It is the engagement and commitment of people that is the heart of philanthropy—what Aristotle called their virtuousness.

Dollars are important; there is no question about that. But the dollars themselves are only the shadow of the deeper reality. Where individual passion and leadership flow in a civil society, engagement will follow. And where engagement is to be found, philanthropy will flower.

Note

1. *Giving and Volunteering in the United States.* (Washington, DC: The Independent Sector, 2001), 10.

CHAPTER 3

Philanthropy within Financial Structures

Defining Overall Nonprofit Revenue

Simplicity does not precede complexity, it follows it.
Alan J. Perlis, 1922–1990[1]

It is important to recognize that economic crisis does affect nonprofit finances. It is unrealistic to believe otherwise, both because nonprofits are, in fact, economic actors and because those who support them do so with discretionary earned income or assets. There is no question that the global economic free-fall of 2007 to 2009 both reduced nonprofit markets for goods and services and strained philanthropic giving. As Chapter 6, "Does the Economy Matter?," will demonstrate, however, the economic relationship is not simple. Preparing to understand that relationship, and developing strategies for revenue stabilization in stuttering economies, requires understanding the structure of nonprofit revenue itself.

Thematic Summary

Generalizations reveal little about the realities of nonprofit finance and, hence, can provide little guidance in the formulation of financial strategies in challenged economies. Practical strategies unfortunately must begin with the reality of complexity. Much has changed in the nonprofit sector in the last two decades. That change must be understood and accommodated in the development of strategy.

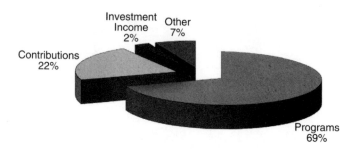

EXHIBIT 3.1 Structure of Public Charity Revenue, 2004
Source: Arnsberger 2008.

In general, U.S. nonprofits are more highly dependent on program and service fees than on private contributions for their financial stability. Comparisons over time are difficult because accounting procedures have changed the way in which membership fees are treated for purposes of tax reporting. Nevertheless, compared to 25 years ago, nonprofits have increased their reliance on fees for service and decreased their reliance on private contributions, which now account for about 22 percent of revenues.[2] As seen in Exhibit 3.1, nearly 70 percent of nonprofit revenue now comes from program services and fees.

In the two-decade period from 1985 to 2004, an Internal Revenue Service sampling of nonprofits found that total inflation-adjusted revenue increased by 173 percent but, as shown in Exhibit 3.2, the rate of increase of program and service fees outpaced the rate of growth of private contributions 204 percent to 183 percent.[3] A study by the Aspen Institute also found that fees and charges represented more than half of the growth in nonprofit revenues in the last 20 years.[4]

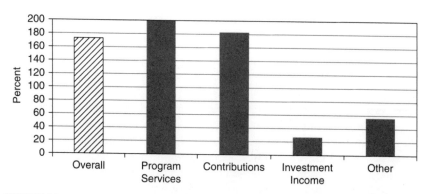

EXHIBIT 3.2 Percent Increase in Public Charity Revenue by Source, 1985–2004
Source: IRS.

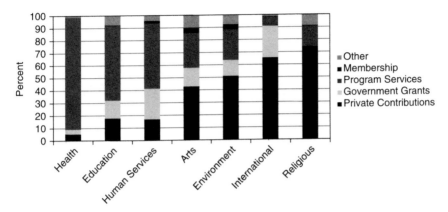

EXHIBIT 3.3 Public Charity Revenue Structure by Sector, 2002

Source: IRS.

Given the wide diversity of organizational size and type in the sector, however, generalizations reveal little about the realities of nonprofit finance and can provide little guidance in the formulation of financial strategies in challenged economies. We must parse the financial sentence much more deeply if strategy is to be formed.

Differences are, to some extent, a function of size and a function of the economic or social sector of which they are a part. In general, smaller nonprofits in sectors for which there has not emerged a "market" for goods and services are much more highly dependent on private contributions than larger nonprofits whose goods or services find a demand in the services market. So, for example, as noted in Exhibit 3.3, health-care organizations that charge service fees are much less dependent on private contributions than are international development or religious organizations.

Sectoral Distinctions and Revenue Structure

If the data are subdivided by sector, the gross distinctions can be immediately perceived. Public charities overall rely on private philanthropy for 22 percent of their revenues, but organizations in the arts, environment, international relief, and religion (to the extent we can judge, given that most do not have to report to the IRS) are much more dependent on philanthropy. Between 40 percent and 70 percent of revenue comes from private contributions. A deeper examination of sector groupings clarifies the extent of the differences and, therefore, the need for revenue strategy to be sensitive to financial structure.

Health

As a sector overall, health is by far the least revenue-dependent on private contributions. This is to be expected because "health organizations" are dominated by hospitals and other service provision institutions. Reimbursement for services is the driving force in the revenue health of this sector, which, in turn, means that public finance policy is the revenue king. In health care overall, the combination of Medicare and Medicaid account for 33.8 percent of health-care expenditures.[5] In hospitals, these two government payment sources account for nearly 60 percent of patient revenue.[6] When a financial downturn includes a severe credit retraction—as did that of 2008–2009—economic effects are also passed onto hospital finance through increased interest expenses for bonds, changed collateral requirements, and difficulty in refinancing debt. Consequently, the financial health of hospitals—even in times of economic distress—is more heavily dependent on public health-care policy and especially on fiscal decisions about health service reimbursement budgets—and more dependent on the credit markets than on the decisions of individual philanthropists.

That does not mean, however, that philanthropy is unimportant. For smaller health-care organizations, philanthropy is critical—a topic explored later in this chapter. Even in large health-care institutions, philanthropy plays a role that is much larger than the size of its dollar in the institutional budget. The philanthropic dollar is unique in two ways: (1) It can be planning-driven and (2) it can be needs-driven.

First, the philanthropic dollar is not tied to current public policy but rather to future visions. It can be solicited and allocated to serve the specific plans of a health-care institution at a particular point in time or relative to disease control over the long haul.

The philanthropic dollar flows to future desires for growth and quality improvement of an institution. The reimbursement dollar allows an institution to avoid financial starvation; the philanthropic dollar allows an institution to evolve and mature. It is, therefore, an exceedingly important resource. Left to subsist on reimbursement alone, health-care institutions can only tread water in the increasingly deep waters of an aging population, complex disease patterns, and rapid scientific advance. Reimbursement will allow institutions to provide services (often some, but not all, services) within regulated and inflexible cost-per-service parameters. That service reimbursement dollar, however, rarely allows them to expand, deepen, or innovate in service delivery. Without philanthropy, the result is a system of health-care institutions that gradually cave into themselves, narrowing services, meeting fewer needs, eroding quality.

There is ample evidence of the effect of such financial constraints. Large urban public hospitals, nearly entirely dependent on public reimbursement,

The Importance of Long-Term Partnerships: The Case of Secure the Future

For most nonprofits, survival in tough or uncertain times depends in large part on history, on the types of funders you have attracted over the years, how you have engaged them as part of your strategy, and how they themselves have benefited from the partnership. Here at the Bristol-Myers Squibb Foundation, our goal always has been to work with organizations we fund to do at least three things: First, to help them become more self-sufficient, by building their capacity so that they can attract additional funding—with or without us. Second, to encourage grantees to focus less on short-term cash gifts or grants and instead to work together to create a strategic vision of where, together, we want a program to go and how to get there using a variety of assets we may have available, including cash, but also including in-kind services or knowledge transfers. And third, to act as a catalyst for action by funding innovative approaches that can, by their novel nature, attract additional funding/partners and, most important, evolve to make a longer-term impact.

Our Secure the Future program—a comprehensive initiative that we began 10 years ago that today focuses on vulnerable populations affected by the HIV/AIDS pandemic in 16 countries in Africa—is an example of how we turn those aspirations into actions. Over the years, we have supported this program—one that addresses great unmet needs in this region—by funding more than 200 grants and projects with some $150 million. But early on, we learned the importance of using our own core capabilities to expand the impact of that funding. For instance, we provided services from our then auditor—PricewaterhouseCoopers—to help our small African grantees gain greater financial and managerial skills. We transferred our clinical trial expertise to local health organizations so that they could better administer and gather necessary data from various clinical programs around HIV/AIDS. And we focused on partnerships with groups on the ground in Africa to create sustainable and replicable projects over time.

And while Secure the Future itself has continued to transform, now serving as a technical resource for governments and communities to adapt or replicate the models created over the years, the partnerships with our grantees have continued. That's because, from the outset, we were working together toward a common goal. In that process, we engaged partners whose missions complemented or supported shared

(Continued)

(Continued)

objectives. So the relationships have continued as we all continue to work together toward changing the face of HIV/AIDS in Africa. This is very different from models of grant making that are focused solely on single or several cash contributions.

We share mutual goals with our grant recipients: to make each other better, create sustainable change, and build capacity for the future. They accept our funding, but more than that, they remain committed to our partnership in order to create a longer-term vision of change.

John Damonti
President
Bristol-Myers Squibb Foundation

are some of the most problematic health-care providers in the country. Their options for quality improvement are limited. Indeed, their options for expanding the range of services needed to meet even the basic but still complex health-care needs of a growing and ethnically diversifying population are severely bounded by public resource availability. As government institutions, they have neither the organizational freedom nor the private constituencies to develop philanthropic options. As a result, they struggle and often wither.

In contrast, robust private nonprofit health-care institutions have the ability to solicit and invest philanthropic dollars in service expansion, quality, and innovation apart from the financial and budgetary constraints imposed by reimbursement rates. The clear utility of such community commitment of philanthropy to health-care improvement has led many public hospitals to create affiliated but private nonprofit foundations to gather in private philanthropy as a means to service improvement. This is obviously not a straightforward task. Not only must the new entity compete for local philanthropic attention relative to other, older community nonprofits but it must create a culture of fund-raising within hospital management perhaps long oriented to public resources and public policy. The latter can be a particular problem. All culture is learned. Established institutional cultures are well learned and deeply embedded over decades. New cultures—the entrepreneurial flexibility required of philanthropic fund-raising—do not easily supplant the old. Nevertheless, the pace of change in health care and the rising demands of an aging population place a premium on service innovation. And it is the philanthropic dollar—not the regulated reimbursement dollar—that holds the promise of investment innovation for health-care service providers.

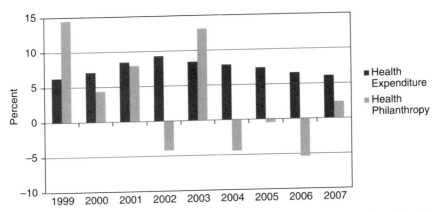

EXHIBIT 3.4 Year-over-Year Change in Health-Care Costs Compared to Health Philanthropy, 1999–2007

Sources: Expenditures: U.S. Centers for Medicare and Medicaid Services; Philanthropy: Giving USA.

The second unique role of the philanthropic dollar in health care—its ability to align with need—is also important. As economies falter and unemployment grows, service providers are faced with growing ranks of the under- or uninsured. The American Hospital Association estimates that every 1 percent increase in unemployment leads to a loss of employer-sponsored coverage for 2.5 million employees and dependents.[7] It is the philanthropic dollar that allows health care to compensate not just for the uninsured but also to enable services to the underinsured for services that are life-saving but not included in private or public reimbursement.

With the 2008–2009 recession driving unemployment rates to or near double-digit levels in some communities, the rolls of the under- and uninsured have risen rapidly. The stress on the philanthropic dollar can be extreme. As shown in Exhibit 3.4, even in relatively normal economic times, the rate of cost inflation in health care has exceeded the rate of increase in health-care philanthropy in all but two of the last nine years. The philanthropic dollar in health care has become extremely dear. The rise in the number of patients requiring financial support to pay for care in a stressed economy puts even more pressure on, and lends even more value to, that dollar.

Education

The education sector is second, after health care, in its reliance on program service revenue for financial support. For private education institutions, it is tuition that drives the financial bus. For public institutions, it is government budgets—state and federal—that pipe the financial tune.

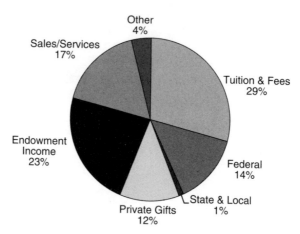

EXHIBIT 3.5 Sources of Revenue—Private Higher Education, 2006
Source: Chronicle of Higher Education.

For both private and public institutions, however, philanthropy, while arithmetically a small part of budgets, plays much the same outsized role, relative to its revenue portion, as it does in health care.

In private higher education, as noted in Exhibit 3.5, more than a third of all revenue comes from private gifts and the income from privately donated endowments. Even in the wealthiest private education institutions, private philanthropy is critical. At Harvard University, the $1.2 billion in distributions from endowment in the 2007–2008 academic year accounted for 34.5 percent of university revenue. Capital distributions accounted for another $400 million, or just more than 11 percent of revenue. A decade ago, such distributions accounted for 23 percent of revenue.[8] Severe economic crisis and falling endowment levels can, therefore, seriously impact the operating revenue streams of private higher education.

In public education, philanthropy is also critical. In public higher education institutions, the combination of income from endowments and private contributions (largely through affiliated foundations) represents 6 percent. Its importance, however, is far in excess of its proportional size. In these schools, state and local government budget support represents nearly 40 percent of revenues. With public budgets squeezed in an economic downturn, and tuitions constrained by public regulation, public universities have few places to turn except to private contributions to keep their budgets whole.

Private contributions have also become a factor in public K–12 education. The number of affiliated private foundations created to raise private funds for K–12 public schools or school systems has increased sixfold in the last decade. There are now more than 1,200 organizations supporting their local schools that touch 11 million students in 32 states and the District of Columbia.[9]

At times of economic peril, therefore, the price that education pays in reductions in philanthropy is not the existence of educational institutions. There will always be demand for private education, and there will always be legal requirements for public budgets to provide public education. Rather, the price is the combination of quality and access. Education relies on philanthropy for two assets, both of which are at a premium when economies are facing hard times and both of which are misunderstood if seen merely in terms of the portion of the educational dollar accounted for by private philanthropy.

First, private philanthropy enables educational institutions to invest and innovate on the edges of knowledge, to build the capacity—whether measured in terms of infrastructure, technology, or people—to keep U.S. institutions in the forefront of change. This is true in private education settings, but it is increasingly also true in public education. It is this philanthropic role in public education that is perhaps the most critical in times of economic crisis because the state and local budgets that support public institutions—universities, community colleges, high schools, and elementary schools—are the first to come under fiscal stress. Without private philanthropy, public education institutions have little if any protection from the necessary cutbacks in public budgets.

The second educational role is to enable a diverse United States to access education. As economies sink, more and more students need financial assistance. And the existing financial assistance must be spread across not only those from the poorest sectors of U.S. society, but those from the middle class. Without private philanthropy, access to quality education, always a financial challenge, would narrow even further. Hence, educational institutions in economically challenging times must search for strategies not only to maintain philanthropic giving, but even to increase that giving. Rising demand for aid requires increased resources, placing educational institutions at a vortex of challenge far in excess of the 17 percent of their overall revenues represented by private contributions.

Human Services

The human services sector also shows a major reliance on program services revenue rather than private philanthropy. In the past two decades, the shift in public policy to private provision of social services through public budget payments has strengthened the role of public finance in social service nonprofit viability. In 2001, an estimated $115 billion in direct federal payments flowed to nonprofits, and another $85 billion flowed indirectly from the federal government to nonprofits through state and local governments.[10] Federal support to nonprofits increased more than 230 percent in inflation-adjusted dollars from 1980 to 2004.[11]

Although resource flows through Medicare represent a significant portion of the direct federal flows, federal monies, together with state and local monies, are also critical to service provision in human service areas, such as child welfare, day care, substance abuse, homelessness, and the like. Indeed, human services organizations rely on government grants and contracts for services for more than three-quarters of their income.

This means that an economic downturn represents a fiscal, even if not primarily a philanthropic, problem for human services organizations. This is a very different problem for human service organizations than, for example, for public education. In education, state fiscal constraints may erode education budgets. Nevertheless, much of the cost structure is already sunk—the buildings exist, teachers are on payroll, professors have tenure, so the reductions can crimp growth and evolution but do not threaten institutions.

In the human services sector, in contrast, there are few sunk investments of public funds. Payments are for immediate services. These payments can be reduced without burden to previous public infrastructure or personnel investments. The nonprofit human services sector exists apart from government investment in such infrastructure. The temptation to reduce support carries no costs in terms of past investments or recurring labor or payroll commitments. Therefore, the effect of an economic downturn on human services organizations has potentially more serious public financing implications than in education or health care.

Caught up in the effects of such a fiscal crisis, with grants and service contracts seriously constrained, human services nonprofits need to turn with force to private support. After decades of growing government funds flows, there is now a strategy problem. Years of necessarily attending to the structures and processes required for government support of services have often weakened the systems and structures required to nurture and cultivate private philanthropic and community resources.

First, many human services agencies may lack deep volunteer leadership, either on their boards or in their program service ranks. Building pathways to leadership and community philanthropy, then, requires basic spadework. This spadework is the slow, hard work required of all nonprofits. It takes time. The good news is that a single individual, committed and passionate, can make a watershed difference. Volunteer leadership need not start with a board of 40; it can start with a single individual who becomes the constant fire underneath that board, and the overall nonprofit, keeping it constantly focused on moving forward, committing his or her own resources and bringing to the side of the organization peers who will do the same.

Of course, fiscal crisis makes time scarce. Time to find and recruit a passionate volunteer leader or leaders is often allocated to other, seemingly more important priorities. But in fiscal crisis, there is no more important priority. Only the engagement of passionate leaders can steady the rudder when financial seas are rough. If those leaders are not in place before the storm hits—as they often are not in the human services nonprofits—then the priority must be on finding and bringing them on board immediately.

Second, the demand for services in crisis economies escalates rapidly. The reality of cutbacks in public budgets reduces neither demand nor public expectations that demand will be met. Human service nonprofits in economic crisis are expected to step into the societal breech. They cannot simply suspend operations in order to address revenue issues and realign sources of financial support. They must, in effect, rewire the house while all the lights are on. This is clearly a complex proposition. Success requires a combination of speed and dexterity in financing strategy, flexible budgeting, an expanded use of volunteers, aggressive deployment of a community communications program, and skilled and sophisticated management. This combination of assets is often more than human services nonprofits— especially small nonprofits—can muster in an economic crisis. Crisis confronts many small human services nonprofits with the harsh reality of limited systems capacity.

Chapters 8 and 9 of this volume will address practical pathways to cope with these strategic issues, as well as suggest core principles for producing organizational strength through the management of revenues in economic hard times. Suffice for now to say that economic crisis poses perhaps the greatest challenges in the human services sector.

Philanthropy-Dependent Sectors

As noted above, many categories of nonprofits are more dependent on private philanthropy than public financing and face a more concentrated problem of private contributions maintenance in a stressed economy. Arts organizations, international relief and development nonprofits, environmental organizations, and religiously affiliated institutions all depend on private philanthropy for 40 percent or more of their revenue.

Clearly, the revenue adjustment options for these organizations are more limited, and the need to attend closely to their volunteer leadership and their support base is critical in an economic crisis.

Let us take two examples to make the point, one from the arts and one from the environment.

As shown in Exhibit 3.6, overall, nonprofit arts organizations derive 40 percent of their income from private contributions and another 50 percent from earned income, some portion of which is derived from ticket sales,

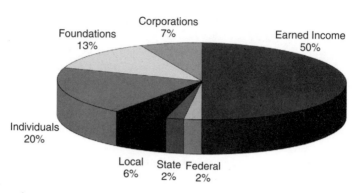

EXHIBIT 3.6 Revenue Sources of Arts Organizations, 2004
Source: National Endowment for the Arts, 2004.

admissions, and the like.[12] About 20 percent of total contributions (or half of private support) comes from individuals. Since individuals also attend performances, buy napkins, and wander museum galleries, let us conservatively say that half of the earned income is also from individuals. For arts organizations, then, perhaps 45 percent of total income is traceable to individual behavior. Therefore, in an economic crisis, the importance of individual giving and individual organizational support is a critical component of revenue strategy for arts organizations in a way that it is not for, let us say, hospitals. It is harder for the individual to delay the gall bladder operation (which is at least partially insured) than it is to substitute popcorn and a home video for a trip to the museum. In turn, the revenue strategy for arts organizations may have very different components and very different communications elements than for health-care providers. One size will not fit all.

The environment provides a second example. The last decade has seen nearly a 50 percent growth in the number of environmental nonprofits and more than a doubling of their revenue.[13] Yet polls show that only 40 percent of those who identify with an environmental cause actually donate to an environment nonprofit.[14] Although donations to the environment come overwhelmingly from upper-income Americans, it is the young who show the most concern for and commitment to the sector.[15] In an economic crisis, then, environmental organizations face a complex equation. More wealthy supporters may be hardhit in terms of incomes and donations, and the youth with whom issues resonate most deeply are not yet significant financial donors.

Making a generational leap in support over turbulent economic waters will require an emphasis on communications and outreach using tools (e.g., technologies) that may not be equally robust for, let us say, soup kitchens.

Again, the point here is that revenue strategies in economic hard times must reflect the realities and specifics of organizational revenue structure and the demographics of the support base.

Size Distinctions and Revenue Structure

If there are clear sectoral differences in nonprofit revenue structure—and so clear strategy distinctions to be made in how to adjust philanthropic solicitation in a crisis economy—are there size differences? Is philanthropic vulnerability within revenue structure different for the large compared to the small? Who needs to worry most in economic crisis?

It is important to understand the degree of revenue concentration within the nonprofit sector. As noted earlier, the term "nonprofit" is an umbrella sheltering a wide range of organizations. This is especially true in terms of size. Exhibits 3.7 and 3.8 illustrate the point. Large organizations (those with more than $10 billion in assets) represent between 5 percent and 10 percent of nonprofit organizations, depending on sector, but between 50 percent and 90 percent of all private contributions and between 40 percent and 90 percent of all program service fees. Hence, any generalities about nonprofit strategy in economic hard times must take into account the degree to which revenue itself is concentrated in a minority of large organizations.

In general, it is true that large nonprofits are less dependent on private contributions than small organizations. As noted in Exhibits 3.9 and 3.10,

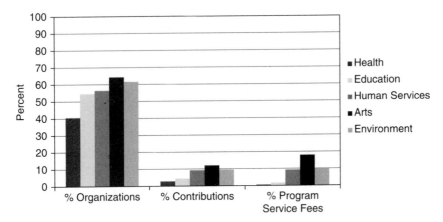

EXHIBIT 3.7 Small Organization Distribution (Assets Less than $500 Million), 2002
Source: IRS.

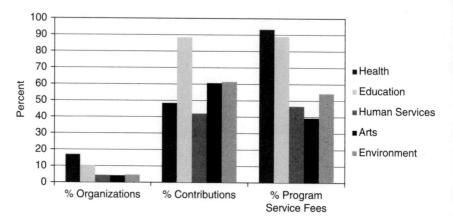

EXHIBIT 3.8 Large Nonprofit Concentration by Sector (Assets Greater than $10 Billion), 2002

Source: IRS.

this is particularly true in the health and education sectors, where the overwhelming importance of service reimbursements and tuition in hospitals and colleges/universities skews the sectoral data significantly.

However, the picture is actually more complex. Smaller arts organizations and smaller environmental nonprofits are actually less dependent on private contributions than are their larger counterparts. In smaller healthcare and education nonprofits, on the other hand, private philanthropy plays a much more significant role than in large organizations. Indeed, for

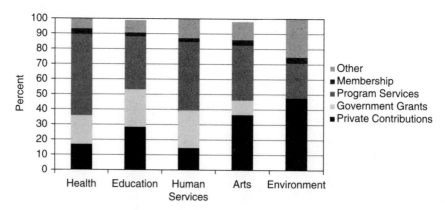

EXHIBIT 3.9 Revenue Structure of Smaller Nonprofits by Sector (Assets Less than $500 Million), 2002

Source: IRS.

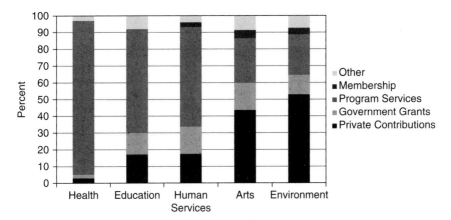

EXHIBIT 3.10 Revenue Structure of Large Nonprofits (Assets Greater than $10 Billion), 2002

Source: IRS.

smaller educational institutions, private contributions are twice as important in revenue structure as they are in large institutions.

For education and health-care organizations, size provides a particular challenge. Smaller organizations represent 55 percent and 40 percent, respectively, of the nonprofits in the sector, but less than 10 percent of all private contributions in the sector. Yet, the smaller the organization, the more important private contributions. In a crisis economy, the difficult question is how to develop a strategy for a significant part of the sector that maximizes its small portion of the total available contributions pie in order to continue its mission.

Summary: The Prerequisite for Strategy Refinement in Hard Times

Revenue strategies for nonprofits in difficult economic times must accommodate two realities about finance in the nonprofit sector. The first is complexity; the second is the convergence of interests between funders and nonprofits.

Complexity

Complexity means that one size does not and will not fit all. The nature of the private contributions problem faced by different types of nonprofits and different sizes of nonprofits will be different. The nature of the

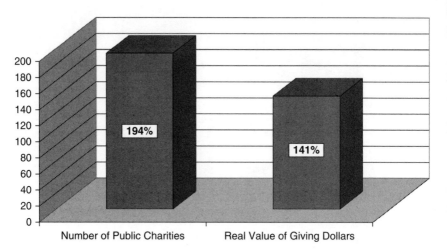

EXHIBIT 3.11 Percent Growth in Nonprofits and Philanthropy, 1982–2007
Source: Giving USA and the National Center for Charitable Statistics.

solution, therefore, will also be different. Strategies to survive, and even
be strengthened by, economic challenges need to be built on fundamental principles of community and leadership commitment to a nonprofit's
mission and services, and be flexible to accommodate the specific characteristics of the structure of revenue that drive toward nonprofit financial
sustainability.

The refinement of strategy to accommodate organizational diversity is
critical. As shown in Exhibit 3.11, the rate of growth in the number of nonprofit institutions in the United States has outstripped the rate of growth
in inflation-adjusted philanthropy. Even as philanthropy has grown, the
philanthropic dollar is becoming dearer. This has been the case in sectors
such as health care for the last decade, even apart from economic challenge. An economic downturn only magnifies this preexisting competition
for scarce resources. In the intense and anxiety-filled environment of economic crisis, clear, purposeful, and highly specific strategy is essential to
success.

Convergence

The relationship between philanthropist and nonprofit is changing. Although
it is true that purely expressive philanthropy—donations that reflect concern
and only concern for good works—is still a part of giving, increasingly philanthropists want engagement in the strategies and works of the nonprofits

they support. Philanthropic revenue no longer comes merely as a check in the mail. It comes with the skills, intellect, and interests of the donor attached. Nonprofits and donors are under one umbrella, not separated by programmatic and management walls.

The refinement of strategy must take this changed relationship into account because it affects not simply the terms of the resource exchange but the management of the nonprofit itself, its culture, and its mechanisms for communication with and engagement of donors. At the staff and management level, such permeability to philanthropic engagement can be difficult because it is perceived as devaluing internal expertise and program control. But it is increasingly a part of the philanthropic "terms of trade" between philanthropists and the nonprofit sector, and revenue strategy must accommodate this and ensure that revenue, program, and management strategy all blend to encourage, and even celebrate, engagement.

Notes

1. Alan J. Perlis was a mathematician and computer scientist whose one-sentence epigrams, written late in his career at Yale University, sum up all that he learned about mastering the complexity of programming.

2. P. Arnsberger. "A History of the Tax-Exempt Sector: An SOI Perspective." *Statistics of Income Bulletin* (Winter 2008).

3. Ibid.

4. "The Nonprofit Sector and the Market: Opportunities and Challenges." The Aspen Institute, 2006.

5. Centers for Medicare and Medicaid Services, Office of the Actuary, 2006, released in January 2008.

6. "Report on the Economic Crisis: Initial Impact on Hospitals." American Hospital Association (November 2008), 20.

7. Ibid., 11.

8. "University Endowments: The Gathering Storm." *Harvard Magazine,* November 7, 2008.

9. "Who Helps Public Schools: A Portrait of Local Education Funds, 1991–2002." The Urban Institute (November 2003).

10. "Nonprofit Sector: Increasing Numbers and Key Role in Delivering Federal Services." Statement of Stanley J. Czerwinski, Director of Strategic Issues, U.S. Government Accounting Office to the Subcommittee on Oversight, Committee on Ways and Means, U.S. House of Representatives, July 24, 2007, 7.

11. Ibid.

12. S. Raymond, "The Arts in America: Whence the Money?" in S. Raymond, *A Briefing on Trends in Philanthropy and the Arts*. (New York: Changing Our World, Inc. 2007), 19–25.

13. *Giving USA* 2008. Glenville, IL: Giving USA Foundation, 2009.

14. "Toward an Ecological Majority," *American Environics*, 2006.

15. S. Raymond, "Structure of the Environmental Nonprofit Sector: Will the Young Make a Difference?" in S. Raymond, *A Briefing on the Impact of Philanthropy in the Environment* (New York: Changing Our World, Inc., 2008), 20–25.

CHAPTER 4

Emerging Nonprofit Revenue Parameters

Accommodating Change in the Interests of Stability

It is difficult to make predictions, especially about the future.
Yogi Berra

A fter reviewing the complexity of existing revenue structure in the non-profit sector, it is important also to understand that strategy for future economic crisis must be informed by the past but must accommodate the future. Although it is true that, as Yogi Berra so wisely observed, prediction is often an art not a science; it is also clear that the future will not be like the past. Much is changing in the operating environment of nonprofits. First of all, the very definition of "nonprofit" is evolving to encompass many types of organizational responses to societal needs. In addition, globalization, technological innovations, and markedly shifting demographics will all alter both the environment within which nonprofits work and provide both constraints on and opportunities for nonprofit revenue strategy. The purpose here is not to provide an exhaustive treatment of each but to illustrate how fundamental changes outside of the nonprofit sector can and will impact revenues. The four changes together thus create the absolute necessity for sophisticated revenue strategy in challenging economic times.

Thematic Summary

Fundamental changes outside of the nonprofit sector can and will impact revenue. All of these changes reflect the evolution of societies and economies. They are beyond the control of the sector, but the result will be an absolute necessity for sophisticated strategy within the sector. All revenue strategy must constantly accommodate and, indeed, capitalize on changes in a nonprofit's operating environment. The organization that stands still falls behind.

The Definition of a "Nonprofit"

The entire operating environment of the nonprofit sector is changing. Historically, "nonprofits" were largely to be found where social problems were intractable, where the concept of "markets" did not apply, and where few except the government held any organizational responsibility. Orphanages, soup kitchens, and homeless shelters all were the face of the nonprofit sector. Indeed, as noted in Chapter 1, "Beginning at the Beginning," the rationale for tax exemption in the first place was that nonprofits perform duties that would otherwise have to redound to government budgets.

Dual Identity: The Intersections between Charity and Markets

The intersection between nonprofits and the societal commons has changed. Nonprofits still serve purely charitable roles, but they are now also part of multi-institutional complexes of economic and social responses to societal needs. Examples abound.

Nonprofit hospitals compete with for-profit hospitals for patients and payments. Indeed, consumers now see little quality difference between for-profit and nonprofit hospital providers.[1] For-profit firms have entered the education field, managing public K–12 education schools and even systems. Private equity is investing in higher education, both in companies that sell into the higher education sector and even in acquiring previously nonprofit colleges.[2] Indeed, before the recent stock market retraction, the stock index of publicly traded education companies had increased sixfold since 1999.[3]

Nonprofits must worry not just about competition for private donor contributions but also about changes in the emerging market for relevant goods and services. In effect, many nonprofits increasingly must live in two worlds—that of their charitable mission and that of the commercial market. Two illustrations cast this complexity into bold relief.

Microfinance, once a nonprofit tool for funding nonprofits and individ-ual entrepreneurship, is now very much a commercial tool that flows funds not only to nonprofits but also to all manner of commerce. Thirty years ago, ACCION pioneered the development of microfinance loan programs in Recife, Brazil, and Mohammed Yunus brought it to maturity through the Grameen Bank. He went on to win the Nobel Prize for that effort. Today, there are between 3,000 and 4,000 microfinance funds around the world bringing not just the resources of local financial institutions to societal prob-lems but those of global finance. In 2007, the first microfinance facility was created using global capital markets. The location? Not the United States. Azerbaijan. In many ways, microfinance is a thread that often sews charitable endeavor and commercial capital together in ways that empower problem solving but also requires nonprofits to compete for capital with commercial alternatives.

The rise of unrelated business income in the nonprofit sector provides a second example of how the charitable and commercial markets are blend-ing. "Unrelated business income" extends nonprofit revenue sources beyond income from fees for programs and services. It represents income that is unrelated to a nonprofit's primary tax exempt purpose or is pursued for pur-poses other than furthering its charitable mission. Examples might include rental of educational facilities for other than educational purposes, or sales of goods that do not reflect the charitable activities of the organization.

A tax on such income was enacted in 1950 in response to for-profit corporate claims of unfair competition from tax exempt organizations of all types selling equivalent goods without the burden of taxes.[4] Still, little data is available on nonprofit tax filings until the mid-1980s. Between 1990 and 2004, the number of nonprofits claiming unrelated business income increased by 22 percent, but the inflation-adjusted value of that income increased by 87 percent in 2004 dollars,[5] as noted in Exhibit 4.1, totaling nearly $1 billion.

Public charities report more unrelated business income than any other type of tax exempt organization.[6]

This growing intersection of tax exempt status and markets is of increas-ing concern to public policy and must inform revenue strategy for nonprofits engaged at the overlap of social benefit and commercial markets. When the Mall of America, the nation's largest shopping mall, applies for tax exempt status on the basis of its role as a major tourist attraction, policy eye-brows are understandably raised.[7] But policy makers are reacting to more than such extreme examples. Nonprofit day care facilities, the overwhelm-ing majority of whose enrollees pay fully for services, are seen as unfairly competing with for-profit day care alternatives.[8] Concern over the business revenues of registered public charities is extending into constellations of institutions that have long enjoyed widely acknowledged nonprofit status. In

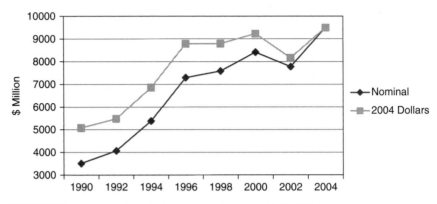

EXHIBIT 4.1 Nonprofit Unrelated Business Income, 1990–2004

Source: IRS.

October 2008, for example, the Internal Revenue Service announced plans to distribute a 33-page questionnaire to 400 public and private colleges as part of its assessment of compliance with nonprofits status requirements. Part of the concern was the reporting of unrelated business income from activities not directly related to the charitable or educational missions of the colleges.[9]

Public policy interests are not simply at the level of the federal government. State and local governments are also vested in nonprofit revenue structure both from an income tax point of view and from a property tax point of view. Indeed, in some communities, up to 50 percent of property is off the tax roles due to exemption, placing pressure on property tax rates for residents. A crisis economy that confronts states and cities with eroding budgetary capacity can be expected to result in those same political entities looking for dimes anywhere they can, including in the tax exempt status of nonprofits.

At the intersection of charity and markets, the problems of an economic downturn thus can present nonprofits with a double-edged financial sword, and solutions, however rational financially, can run afoul of public budgetary interests. On the one hand, economic downturns create challenges for maintaining levels of private contributions. This is true for most nonprofits. For those nonprofits that have diversified their revenue streams into other more "market"-driven areas, the economic downturn intensifies the revenue effect. Not only are individual donations at risk, but consumer spending falls. Both private voluntary and market revenue streams contract.

For those who have attempted to stabilize finance through diversification into unrelated business areas, strategy for nonprofit finance in a crisis economy requires a complex calculus of assessing and restoring both voluntary and market behavior of individuals.

"Social" Markets

A second dimension of this redefinition of the nonprofit sector with revenue strategy implications in a crisis economy is the "marketization" of the societal commons. In some areas of the societal commons, what has historically been a matter of charitable endeavor is now a matter of market growth. As these markets grow and expand, they fundamentally change the roles and potential for nonprofit endeavor. Nonprofits seeking to cope with and recover from financial crisis must understand how the ground upon which they are standing now is likely to shift in the future. Strategy for today, even strategy for tomorrow, is immaterial where radical change is on the horizon.

This is most obviously typified by the recent evolution of the environmental sector. Total philanthropic giving to environmental nonprofits and causes in 2007 was about $6 billion, a sum that has tripled in the last 20 years. Yet that figure represents only about 2 percent of all philanthropic giving. Private foundations have also nearly doubled the dollar value of their grant making for the environment in the last decade; yet the doubling has moved the needle of dollar value from 4.7 percent of all grant dollars a decade ago to 5 percent today.

In contrast, the total global environment technologies market is $600 billion, 100 times the size of environmental philanthropy.[10] Global investment in new energy technology increased by 60 percent between 2006 and 2007, and totals nearly $150 billion, about two-thirds of which is invested in wind and biofuels, as noted in Exhibit 4.2. New strategies pervade the societal commons in resolving environmental problems. Policy makers have developed frameworks for trading pollution rights, turning environmental qualities into commodities. Once an environmental dimension becomes a

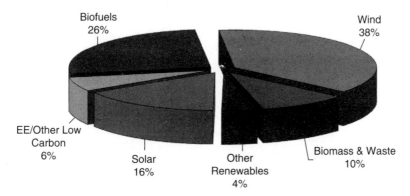

EXHIBIT 4.2 Global Investment in Sustainable Energy by Technology, 2006
Source: SEFI, New Energy Finance.

commodity, there is a market for its sale and purchase. In 1990, the Environmental Protection Agency (EPA) set an overall limit on sulfur dioxide emissions but allowed companies to trade among themselves to meet these limits. Today, the market for sulfur dioxide emissions is valued at $4 billion, and SO_2 emissions are used as collateral for swapping other pollutants. What has been the result? In the United States, SO_2 emissions are expected to fall to half their 1980 levels by 2010. Some analysts expect the pollutant commodities market to have a valuation of $1 trillion by 2012.[11]

Does this mean that a nonprofit in a sector that is being transformed into a market has no future? No, but it does mean that programming within such a nonprofit must accommodate the change. Therefore, revenue strategies that support programming must be equally aware of the nonprofit's role in a marketized social sector and triangulate strategy to take advantage of the robustness of new economic actors. Such rapidly changing sectors and definitions hold promise for producing both new philanthropic resources and new types of nonprofit-for-profit partnerships. But those opportunities will not be effectuated without strategy. Revenue strategy in these new operating environments needs to purposefully seek to establish creative partnerships on the cusp of change.

Globalization of Economies, Leadership, and Philanthropy

Volumes have been written on the degree to which the world is increasingly tightly knit. Only a few highlights are needed to make the point. Global trade now accounts for more than 25 percent of global gross domestic product (GDP), compared to just 7 percent in 1965. An economic sneeze in Shanghai can cause a cold in St. Louis and double pneumonia in Sao Paulo.

The nonprofit sector itself has spread globally. As shown in Exhibit 4.3, outside of North America, there are nearly as many nonprofits in Africa as

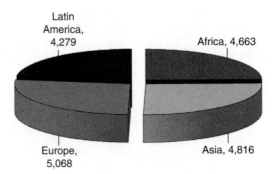

Latin America, 4,279
Africa, 4,663
Europe, 5,068
Asia, 4,816

EXHIBIT 4.3 Global Distribution of Nonprofits, 2000
Source: Interconnection.

there are in Europe. All nonprofits seek to pursue their own missions, and all compete for resources, including philanthropy. Moreover, they compete for philanthropic resources not just in their own countries and regions but across the globe. Increasingly, nonprofit organizations are establishing "friends of" support groups in multiple countries to gather global financial support for their operations. Americans contribute private philanthropy to the U.S. affiliates of international organizations like the United Nations Food Programme headquartered in Rome, museums like the National Gallery of London, and universities and schools from around the world whose increasing number of alumni from study-abroad programs represent a burgeoning group of globally traveled and internationally educated Americans with a propensity to support institutions abroad. Such "friends of" approaches also benefit from the rising trends of immigration to the United States and the presence of foreign professionals with long-term job commitments in the United States.

This trend both increases philanthropy by attracting more people to giving, and increases local competition for resources.

Leadership and public interest are also increasingly global. Philanthropy is now a global media topic. Global philanthropic leaders are to be found throughout the world, empowered by the economic growth in China, Brazil, Russia, South Africa, and the like. Recent economic hardship has eroded that wealth, but those who created it are not dead. Their entrepreneurial skills are intact, and their philanthropic leadership will continue as economies recover. Moreover, the citizens of most industrialized countries are increasingly aware of global needs. Americans spend more on international travel than the total gross national product (GNP) of the nation of Bolivia. Study-abroad programs are now an accepted part of the college experience in the United States. Indeed, two-year schools are also starting study-abroad programs, and these schools see a higher portion of minorities studying abroad than do universities.[12] Whole university campuses are linking globally. Awareness and commitment to cause are likely to ignore borders in the minds of future philanthropists.

Technology: The Emergence of Social Networking

The second fundamental change in the nonprofit operating environment is the emergence of social networking. For the last decade, nonprofits have been slowly adopting their revenue strategies to the growing strength of electronic communication. E-philanthropy—or giving online—totaled some $10 billion in 2008.[13] Although this is only about 3 percent of total philanthropic giving, the revenue source is significant for some nonprofits. Heifer International, for example, obtains 28 percent of its contributions through

Building Out from Local Leadership:
The Cambodian Countryside Development Foundation

As a young person aware of the world's crises but with limited resources, I often struggle to find a way to make an impact on the lives of those in need. During a summer in Cambodia, working alongside Cambodian peers training local nonprofits, I found the solution and created the Cambodian Countryside Development Foundation (CCDF).

My time in Cambodia, spent in the villages of "the poor," showed me a side of economic development rarely covered by the media. Too often, stories of poverty depict people as helplessly resigned to the handouts of the Western world. Rarely does the public see an empowered third-world entrepreneur working to lead a life of hope and to provide for his or her community. It was these individuals, indigenous leaders striving to take back *their* country from war and desperation and treating me as family, who inspired the genesis of CCDF.

Moreover, unlike many Western nonprofits, my Cambodian counterparts were starved of resources but striking in their impact. The flow of capital, both philanthropic and commercial, is directed to local entrepreneurs infrequently at best; yet it is these individuals whose knowledge and experience can transform small amounts of capital into profound impact.

Such is the driving force of CCDF. With limited resources and facilitated by today's age of global interconnectivity, CCDF provides microgrants to agricultural, environmental, educational, and microlending projects in rural communities. Providing seed money to emerging nonprofits and social entrepreneurs, CCDF helps them reach the first rung on the ladder toward growing their organizations. As a volunteer organization, nearly all of our funds flow to our partners on the ground—partners whose deep local knowledge, vast social networks, and low overhead costs allow us to make maximum impact with minimum investment.

Josh Moore
Co-Founder and Executive Director
The Cambodian Countryside Development Foundation

online strategies. Moreover, the preference for online giving is not just a characteristic of the very young. A survey of individuals with $100,000 or more in income, or who donate $10,000 or more annually, indicated that between 46 percent and 56 percent of those who give prefer to give online.[14]

Harnessing the Web to Message

With the need growing, competition increasing, and the available funds contracting, CBM has continually looked for mechanisms to cost-effectively reach both existing and new donors and has found success in a variety of Web-based tools.

Although it is easy to consider Web-based activities as a standalone effort, we have been careful to make certain that our Web efforts are consistent with our broader strategic and marketing initiatives. Our initial effort was to focus on the Web as a way to extend our reach and reinforce our message to existing donors. With the demographics of our donor base leaning toward older donors, we were initially concerned about effectively reaching them over the Web. We have since found that a surprising number of these donors are technologically savvy, responding well to our Web site, targeted e-mails that build on our traditional direct mail appeals, and electronic delivery of information/newsletters.

Expanding beyond our traditional donor base, we have also had success through the offering of incentives or promotions via the Web. As an example of success in this area, we recently offered a free mission-related publication via our Web site. This simple offering was picked up by other Web sites that offer free items, like findfreestuff.com, and resulted in almost 5,000 requests—5,000 potential donors who learned of our work through the offering of an item that was inexpensive to produce and deliver (most were delivered electronically).

Evolution of the Web continues, and we are currently examining the benefits of social media and other new Web-based tools to spread our message to new and existing donors. With donations via the Web growing faster than any other donation mechanism, it is clear that Web-based communications and fund-raising will remain an important and integral part of CBM's growth strategy.

Ron Nabors
Chief Executive Officer
CBM-US

There is some indication that e-philanthropy, while an important tool in the nonprofit revenue tool box, may need time to mature. Target Analytics, a division of Blackbaud, Inc., has found that online giving can be a one-time experience. A survey of 24 nonprofits showed that 37 percent of those who gave online never did so again.[15] The need is for continuous investment in the technology and strategy that will forge loyalty with online donors. But investment requires resources, a challenge that is more fully discussed below.

What is striking about the future operating environment, however, is not the fact of e-philanthropy; it is the process by which communication moves through the larger and growing network of electronic systems. Social networking is the modus operandi of the future linkages between individuals and organizations.[16] Social networking will be the means for driving donors to cause-focused nonprofits and, hence, the future pathway for e-philanthropy.

Social networking through such mechanisms as Facebook and MySpace establishes interconnected Internet communities through which individuals "meet" one another and become linked to individuals and organizations with whom they would not otherwise become connected. Between 2007 and 2008 alone, total unique visitors aged 15 and over to social networking sites increased by 25 percent worldwide, and now totals an estimated 580 million people.[17] The internationalization of social networking is particularly striking. As noted in Exhibit 4.4, in a single year, 2007–2008, the number of unique visitors to social networking sites grew by a third in Latin America and by nearly 70 percent in the Middle East and Africa. As shown in Exhibit 4.5, Asia and Europe together account for more than 6 in every 10

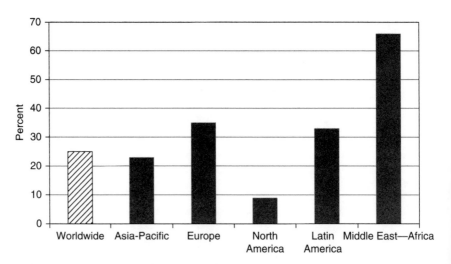

EXHIBIT 4.4 Percent Growth in Social Networking Unique Visitors, June 2007–June 2008

Source: Inside Facebook, 2009.

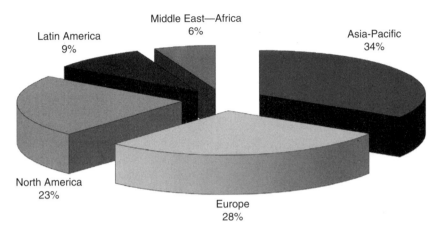

Latin America
9%

Middle East—Africa
6%

Asia-Pacific
34%

North America
23%

Europe
28%

EXHIBIT 4.5 Geographic Distribution of Social Networking Visitors

Source: Inside Facebook, 2009.

unique social network visitors. North America represents less than a quarter of unique visitors. This global reach will increasingly allow nonprofits to access global support, even when they are not able to make an investment in global infrastructure. Again, in economic downturns, this social networking process broadens nonprofit exposure and opens new pathways for private contributions beyond the geographic limits of a nonprofit's physical location. Later sections of this chapter present original data from Future Leaders in Philanthropy on the use of such means among young people with professional and personal interests in philanthropy.

As with all innovation, however, successfully intersecting the arc of change in the electronic environment will not happen automatically. Enhancing revenue stability to withstand economic turmoil through changing electronic means requires purposeful tactics embedded in overall revenue strategies.

Demographics as Destiny

Nonprofits seeking to adjust to, or prepare for the eventuality of, economic challenges must also accommodate themselves to the realities of demographic change. As emphasized in Chapter 2, "Setting the Larger Stage," at the core of a nonprofit's role in civil society is its engagement of individuals in the larger good of their communities. Therefore, people are important, not just as sources of financial support but as the voices and volunteers who root a nonprofit to community. Consequently, understanding what is happening to the characteristics of community is a critical prerequisite for nonprofit strategy.

There are three critical dimensions of this change that must be part of revenue strategies that seek to ensure stability even in economic hard times: (1) aging and longevity, (2) ethnicity, and (3) the characteristics of the younger generations.

Aging and Longevity

It goes without saying that we are an aging nation. The first baby boomer will turn 65 in 2011. The deluge will then begin. By 2030, one in five Americans will have passed their 65th birthday. As shown in Exhibit 4.6, at age 65 the average American can expect to live more than 18 years, well past age 80. Those who reach age 85 can expect to live well past age 90. The Bureau of Census in 2000 found that there were approximately 50,000 Americans over the age of 100, and one-third had no deficits in cognition.

No state and few communities will escape the trend. Nonprofits looking for revenue stability over time and through economic hardship will need to accommodate these realities of aging, not only because they will affect private contributions but because they will affect—indeed they will feed and compound—economic travails themselves. Let us take these issues in reverse order.

First, the relationship between an aging nation and economic challenge is clear. On the one hand, aging will change the structure of dependency in the nation. In 1960, nearly 60 percent of dependents were under the age

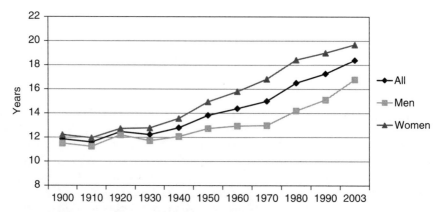

EXHIBIT 4.6 Life Expectancy at Age 65, 1900–2003
Source: Bureau of the Census.

of five; by 2025, nearly 80 percent will be over the age of 65. Not only will the numbers of dependents grow (by 2025, there will be 65 dependents per 100 workers, compared to 51 in 2000) but the cost structure of this dependency will change as well. The social costs (public welfare payments, private subsidies, productivity impacts) of a dependent population over the age of 65 are three times those of childhood dependency. Those over the age of 65 represent 12 percent of the population but account for 35 percent of hospital stays, 47 percent of outpatient visits, and 38 percent of emergency medical responses. Four in five elderly have chronic health conditions and more than half have a disability.

More than half of Americans over the age of 65 live at or below 300 percent of the poverty level; that is, on the edge of needing public assistance funding. Some 45 percent of U.S. senior citizens live on less than $25,000 per year.

The aging of the nation will present a chronic challenge to the U.S. economy and a challenge that nonprofits can expect to be a long-term drag on economic growth absent significant public policy changes or economic productivity innovations.

Second, the aging of U.S. citizens will also affect the structure of private contributions. There are several dimensions to this effect.

On the one hand, it could severely dampen the giving of older Americans. Facing longer lives, the aging population will also face higher costs over longer periods of time. Nearly 70 percent of those reaching age 65 will need some form of long-term care in their lifetimes. Half of the elderly who rent their living space spend more than 30 percent of their income on housing. By 2014, per capita health-care costs will be more than double those of 2000.

Second, longevity will mean that giving will increasingly be a decision that crosses generations. Children will steward parents' resources over long periods of time. When those times include severe economic downturns, the quality of nonprofit communication and strategy will need to be stellar if nonprofit relationships are to survive the dual challenges of economic cycles and aging costs.

In all of this change, trust will be critical. And it is here that additional pause must be taken. The older Americans get, the less they trust the nonprofit sector. Polling questions about the use of nonprofit resources, administrative costs, or general directions of institutions all show the same results. The older Americans get, the more skeptical they are of charitable directions.[18] As shown in Exhibit 4.7, U.S. adults in their 40s begin to doubt that nonprofits are "headed in the right direction" and turn to skepticism. Although it is true that U.S. citizens are generally a skeptical people, that fact provides cold comfort when the trend is extended to the charitable sector.

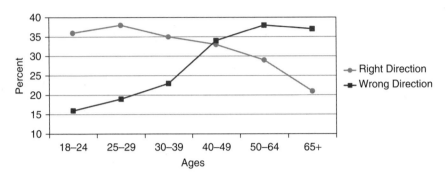

EXHIBIT 4.7 Are Charities Going in the Right Direction or the Wrong Direction?
Source: Harris Interactive.

Nonprofit revenue strategies in challenging economies must understand that as the nation ages, and when fears build in times of economic distress, there may be a fragile floor of trust among older donors. Failed trust will trump all revenue tactics. Nonprofits must closely integrate communications, transparency, accountability, and revenue tactics into a single strategy for reaching out to current and potential supporters. Anything less will run aground on the shoals of skepticism.

Ethnicity

In 1959, immigration accounted for 6 percent of U.S. population growth. Today, it accounts for 40 percent. Between 2008 and 2050, immigrants and their descendents will account for 82 percent of the nation's population growth. The United States is becoming more diverse at every age level.

The U.S. Bureau of the Census estimates that minorities now comprise a third of the U.S. population, and it predicts that minorities will make up the majority of the U.S. population by 2042. More than half of all children will be minority by 2023. Although the percentage of the population in working ages 18 to 64 will fall from 63 percent to 57 percent by 2050 (reinforcing the economic problem of affording an aging population noted above), half of the workforce will be minority. Indeed, between 2001 and 2025, the white adult population aged 40–59 will fall in absolute numbers, while the number of minority adults will increase rapidly.

Rising diversity in the United States is also about the diversity of wealth. About 13 percent of the population is foreign born. But more than a quarter of all of the nation's Nobel Laureates are foreign born, as are nearly a quarter of its venture capital founders, its technology company founders, its scientists and engineers, and even the nation's holders of international

Hispanic Leadership and American Philanthropy

Hispanic Americans are not just the largest ethnic group in the United States, numbering almost 50 million, but one of the most dynamic, vital forces shaping America's future. Younger than other groups, and rapidly gaining economic and political clout, U.S. Hispanics are a vibrant mix of immigrants and families of several U.S.-born generations; the largest group, behind non-Hispanic whites, in the labor force; of an entrepreneurial bent that is fueling the U.S. economic engine; and projected to account for 46 percent of total U.S. population growth over the next two decades.

"Hispanic" does not define country of origin or primary language, only ethnic background. Hispanic consumers have the one of the largest disposable incomes of any minority group in the country, and the U.S. Census predicts a 29 percent growth in the Hispanic population in the next eight years (as opposed to 9 percent generally). Hispanic buying power in 2008 was more than $800 billion (300 percent higher than it was in 1990 and projected to reach $1 trillion by 2010).

Because of differences in per capita income, wealth, demographics, and culture, the spending habits of Hispanics are not the same as those of the average U.S. consumer. The same differences are also prevalent in their philanthropic concerns. Hispanics tend to be attuned to those themes that relate to their own unique reality: education, health, poverty, and community development. They are generous with their causes and are moved emotionally by them.

U.S. nonprofits need to capitalize on the reality of emerging Hispanic economic leadership, yet recognize that these leaders represent different cultures and priorities. The wise nonprofit will first make the effort to understand the Hispanic leader, rather than expect the leader to understand the nonprofit. The nonprofit must present itself and its programs in ways that the Hispanic leaders can trust and to which they can relate in their own ways. The successful nonprofit will come to the leaders, not expect the leaders to come to it. In that way, the nonprofit and the Hispanic leader will begin from a foundation of trust that will smooth the transition to philanthropic support.

Governor Sila M. Calderon
Past Governor of Puerto Rico
Chair, the Center for Puerto Rico

patents.[19] Diversity is no longer just about those whom nonprofits serve; it is about those whose support they seek.

With ethnic change comes religious and cultural change. How people think about philanthropy, what they expect from nonprofits serving their communities, and even their definitions of "community" can be highly colored by culture. Where ethnic composition of populations is changing, revenue strategy must deeply understand and accommodate these differences. Similarly, with growing religious diversity in communities, nonprofits must also understand the dictates of religion as they affect giving and volunteering if nonprofits are to successfully remain vehicles for the engagement of the people in community problem solving. As demographics change in the United States, there is tremendous, and currently largely unmet, need for nonprofits to adjust to and embrace these cultural and religious differences. This is not a matter of "quotas" for staff and board participation. Such superficial answers will quickly be unmasked and will, in any effect, be ineffective. Rather, it is a matter of deeply educating nonprofits about the relevant dimensions of history, culture, and religion that are embedded in a diverse community, and bringing that knowledge not just to services but to strategies for long-term institutional philanthropic support.

Diverse ethnicity within all communities will need to be factored into—indeed will need to fuel—nonprofit revenue strategies. The composition of boards, the composition of fund-raising staff, linguistic capacity, global expertise, institutional knowledge about philanthropy in differing societies and cultures ... all of these elements will be an essential part of strategies for successful nonprofit revenue growth. All are now generally lacking in the nonprofit sector. Strategies to ensure stable revenue streams through future economic challenges must first invest—and invest now—in growing nonprofit organizations into changing ethnicity in America.

The Characteristics of Younger Generations

A survey by the private bank Northern Trust found that the value of gifts from Generation X millionaires aged 28 to 42 was double that of their parents and grandparents.[20] Indeed, a higher portion of college-aged young people volunteer than in the overall adult population.[21] Generosity and consciousness of community needs are not missing from the young. De Tocqueville, quoted at the beginning of this book, would recognize the core of their values, their belief that all things can be improved, however much their world would be a puzzlement to him. But because the core is solid does not mean the ways and means toward the end of social responsibility have not changed.

As noted above, the future younger generations of the United States will be filled with minority young people. But beyond ethnicity, younger

Muslim Philanthropy: Local Tradition Evolves to Global Presence

As the global economy seeks models that are adaptive and embrace viable elements of free enterprise and social responsibility, philanthropy and social entrepreneurship has a role to play in addressing global concerns and challenges. Difficult times call for original responses, and Muslim philanthropy has been one such model that is both sustainable and contributive.

For Muslims, philanthropy is an obligatory part of their faith and is embedded in their sense of self and worldly duty. For centuries, it has encouraged, indeed even mandated, a sense of responsibility to local community and to the Muslim Ummah (community) at large. The mandatory and deep tradition of philanthropy among Muslims is evolving beyond the local to include concerns that are global. Given the Muslim Diaspora's transnational and cosmopolitan nature, the consequent worldview and derived solutions and philanthropy have become global in nature, too.

Given the compulsory disposition of Muslim philanthropy, it has the capacity of being a long-standing and sustainable partner to global philanthropy institutions to further problem solving in areas of development, health, education, and peace building. The development of pioneering philanthropic instruments that are Muslim compliant will add an innovative dimension to the philanthropic sector globally. Muslim philanthropists and Muslim philanthropy can occupy a significant place at the global philanthropy table. Muslim donors and entrepreneurs are powerful forces to be leveraged, especially in this economic climate.

Sara Shroff
Director
Changing Our World, Inc.

generations of U.S. donors will have several characteristics that will need to be part of nonprofit strategy. Indeed, work by the Coalition for New Philanthropy in New York has found that young philanthropists, whatever their ethnicity, show similar motivations and approaches to philanthropy, and that these approaches differ from those of their parents, irrespective of ethnicity.[22] Several of these new characteristics are critical to nonprofit revenue strategy.

First, many Next-Gen givers do not compartmentalize their philanthropy. They see impact on the societal commons as part of their jobs and part of their day-to-day lives. They integrate "philanthropy" into their business concepts, creating or investing in a variety of social enterprises that combine the strategies of private capital finance that lead to scale with the mission of problem solving on the societal commons.[23] This fusion of finance and problem solving leads Next-Gen givers to think less in terms of checkbook philanthropy than in terms of return on investment. A 2009 global survey of philanthropists by Changing Our World and Campden Media of London found that, in marked contrast to older philanthropists, those aged 20 to 35 were more interested in long-term problem solving and more likely to engage in venture philanthropy.[24] They see their giving in the context of the longer arc of their lives and they look for mechanisms for equivalently long-term engagement.

Such a perspective provides a clear challenge to nonprofits. Social problems have multiple roots; programs addressing a single problem often cannot discern changes in that root structure. There are lags between programmatic or service provision and change, lags that can be generational. It is difficult to trace a return on a one-year grant out to a 10- or 20-year change in behavior and social circumstances. Philanthropic fragmentation makes the expectation of return on investment difficult to meet. Nonprofits receive segments of money from large numbers of institutions. The institutions themselves have different interpretations of "return" and often require different measures as evidence. Small grants come with big expectations; large grants come with outsized expectations. The expectations are different, the time frames are different, and only rarely does the grant include funds to actually measure any results, let alone funding sized to the level of expectations. These expectations about return on investment—common but not exclusively held by Next-Gen givers—are not separate from philanthropy. They are part and parcel of the process of giving. Therefore, just as revenue strategy must accommodate changes in nonprofit revenue structure and new modes of funds transfer onto the societal commons, strategy must accommodate these expectations.

Increasingly for nonprofits, getting the money will be fruitless if producing the evidence fails.

Second, as Fulton and Blau have observed, Next-Gen philanthropists have "an interest in finding new ways to get things done with little concern for old habits."[25] Nonprofit age and lineage is of less interest than innovation that breeds success. Next-Gen givers are loyal to problems and causes, not to institutions. Although the vast majority of Next-Gen givers learn about philanthropy from their parents,[26] they do not necessarily adopt either the approaches or interests of older generations.

Third, as noted above, incorporation of technology across a nonprofit's operations is expected. This is not simply a matter of how funds are solicited (i.e., the inclusion of e-philanthropy as a giving option), but how an organization uses technology to achieve efficiency in all communications and networks. Next-Gen givers consider electronic social networks, properly designed and robustly used, to be relationships. Technology is not a mechanism that leads to personal relationships. The communication that remains technologically mediated is, in fact, a relationship.

Accommodating the deep and fundamental role of technology expected by Next-Gen givers is a challenge on two levels. On the one hand, it requires continuous investment. Keeping pace with rapidly changing technologies and communications options is expensive, and the expense requires a constant stream of resource commitment. The resource need cannot be met with a single "capacity building" grant because the solutions of today are almost certainly not going to be up to the task tomorrow. Therefore, meeting Next-Gen expectations requires not a grant but a funded budget line item, a luxury for many nonprofits in the best of times and an impossibility in financial crisis.

On the other hand, nonprofit management—the people in charge of those budgets—is aging. Appreciation of the need for constant technology investments to meet the expectations of tomorrow's philanthropists, and understanding of the nature and power of those technologies, is often lacking. This may continue to be the case. A 2007 survey of the Young Nonprofit Professionals Network indicated that only 55 percent of young professionals in the nonprofit sector intended to stay in the sector for the length of their careers. Even fewer—30 percent—intended to become nonprofit management leaders, and only 9 percent said they were likely to try to head the organization for which they currently work.[27] So, when budgetary demand is greater than resource supply, it is often technology investments that suffer, even though near-term resource tactics can endanger long-term resource strategies. Nonprofits must meet and bond with young people to attract their loyalty and then open themselves and their strategies up to the knowledge, their skills, and ultimately their participation in preparing nonprofits for the technological future.

Fourth, Next-Gen funders expect business plans. They assume that nonprofit organizations are passionate about their missions. But they expect clear and disciplined business plans to get from passion to impact, to lay out a clear pathway and execution plan to get solutions to scale. It is the discipline of the business plan that is primary. It is expected to be fundamental to revenue generation and revenue stability. Fund development—philanthropy—rests within this business plan. Funding strategies neither substitute for business planning nor set its objectives. Rather, business plans must explicitly include both philanthropic goals and alternative scenarios for meeting those goals so that the business and philanthropy are deeply intertwined and work together to weather difficult economies. Business planning is an especially important, even prerequisite, part of revenue strategy in economic hard times because it establishes an organization's clear commitment to sustainable service provision when resources are scarce and competition is intense.

Finally, Next-Gen givers do not see their true value as embodied in their checkbooks. They want to be involved for the long term as knowledgeable and experienced professionals. Because they have become engaged in the prime of their careers, they expect to bring to the nonprofit sector the entirety of their capacity, including their knowledge and skills. Nonprofit revenue strategies, which seek to engage them whether in economic crisis or not, will need to be whole-of-organization strategies not just donation strategies.

From February 4 through February 13, 2009, Future Leaders in Philanthropy (FLiP), a network of young people created in 2002 and interested in and committed to philanthropy, conducted an online survey of young people engaged in philanthropy to assess their attitudes and practices regarding their giving. The survey was specifically designed to illuminate Next-Gen issues discussed in this book. It was promoted through the FLiP Web site and network and through Facebook. The survey generated 125 responses, the vast majority from the United States and Canada. More than 80 percent of respondents were between the ages of 21 and 40, and 93 percent were employed.

Four aspects of the responses were striking.

First, technology clearly matters to their philanthropy. Nearly two-thirds (62.4 percent) prefer to interact with the nonprofits they support via e-mail. Only 5.6 percent wanted to receive regular mail, and only 20 percent wanted to be approached in person.

Nearly every respondent (92.8 percent) had made a donation online; nearly all (89.7 percent) did so because of its convenience even though only a third had given because they were solicited online. That percentage is much higher than the 6 percent of donors who gave online in a 2007 American Express Survey.[28] Of those FLiP survey respondents who had given online, 80 percent had given directly through the nonprofit's Web site; only 49 percent had used an intermediary Web site, such as Donors Choose or Firstgiving.

Second, technology not only facilitates their giving, it facilitates their cause activism. Nearly half (47.2 percent) had created a cause or group on a social network. More than two-thirds (68.3 percent) had forwarded a call-to-action message to family or friends. Amazingly, as shown in Exhibit 4.8, more than three-quarters (76.4 percent) have signed an online petition. Only five respondents had never taken an online action to support a cause or nonprofit.

Third, their issue interests are concentrated, and within those interests impact matters greatly. Their overwhelming interests are in education, social

Young People Ascendant: The FLiP Story

The year was 2005. Three newly minted Changing Our World consultants, fresh out of college, came to a quick conclusion: Their college educations were not quite enough to prepare them for their roles in the spheres of professional fund-raising and grant making. Sure, school taught them to think, and write, and speak—but the nuances of how to make the cut as philanthropic professionals were to be learned in the real world. Luckier than most, these three—Jessica Stannard-Friel, Will Schneider, and Divine Tabios—had each other and other young counterparts with whom to collaborate. But what of their colleagues in development offices and foundations across the country and around the world? What resources and support could be offered to the sole 22-year-old in an office filled with faces over 40, or to the college senior looking to get a break?

The answer: Future Leaders in Philanthropy, or FLiP. This special project of Changing Our World provides time-tested and of-the-moment resources, tips, tricks, and networking opportunities for young fundraisers and grant makers.

Flash forward to 2009. FLiP, is now a dynamic, fast-growing community of young professionals. By working together, FLiP's members further their careers, better serve their organization's mission, and change the world. FLiP is dedicated to creating a network where future leaders can meet, exchange ideas, and contribute to each other's success.

Based in New York, FLiP has expanded its reached globally and now counts thousands of young professionals from diverse locations and backgrounds among its ranks.

FLiP members are able to stay connected through the FLiP Web site, FLiP's Facebook group, and networking events held in New York and select cities around the country. This generation is looking to leverage new media for fund-raising outcomes and to shake up the traditional definition of grant making into a new order of providing time, talent, product, and professional savvy. FLiP's interactive platform is designed to do just that, quickly and seamlessly—young professionals working in the sector.

Elisabeth Anderson
Lyndsay Reville
Divine Tabios
Changing Our World, Inc.

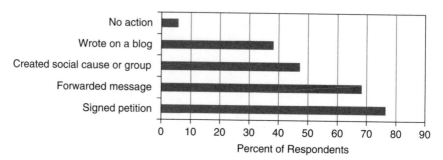

EXHIBIT 4.8 Actions Taken Online by FLiP Survey Respondents
Source: Future Leaders in Philanthropy original survey, 2009.

services, and the arts/humanities. Interestingly, only a third give to the environment and only one in five volunteers give to an environmental cause. International affairs and health care attract equally weak interest. Three things clearly dominate their interest in the nonprofits they support: (1) personal experience, (2) organizational mission, and (3) the availability of measureable and proven impact. A third of respondents ranked "impact" as among the top two considerations influencing their support decisions.

Fourth, they are staring down the 2008–2009 recession. As shown in Exhibit 4.9, nearly 8 in 10 respondents plan to maintain or increase the

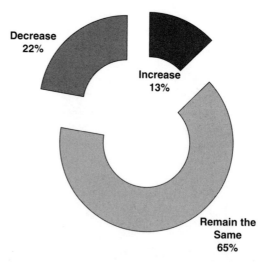

EXHIBIT 4.9 FLiP Survey Respondents Anticipated Giving Reaction to 2009 Economy
Source: Future Leaders in Philanthropy original survey, 2009.

level of their giving in the economic climate of early 2009. Of those who plan to reduce their cash giving, nearly half plan on increasing their online awareness and nearly two in five (39.5 percent) will volunteer more in order to stay involved. These intentions of the young are perhaps in stark contrast to the hesitancy of the wealthy to continue their philanthropy in exceedingly difficult economic times. There is need for the commitment of the young to speak volumes to the commitment of their elders.

The survey indicates that the next generation is and plans to stay involved in philanthropy, and the pathway to their civil society engagement—whether dollars or actions—will be technology.

Summary

Elements of the operating environment of nonprofits are changing markedly, raising new expectations and new opportunities for revenue growth and programmatic effect. Revenue strategies in economic crisis cannot simply ignore these changes. Economies under stress may change the needs of nonprofits and even the propensity of people to give. But they may not change the fundamental characteristics and expectations of those who do give. Nonprofit strategies, even as they seek to cultivate and capitalize on traditional and new funding strategies, must accommodate the evolving views and characteristics of philanthropists themselves.

Notes

1. M. Schlesinger, S. Mitchell, and B. H. Gray. "Public Expectations of Nonprofit and For-Profit Ownership in American Medicine: Clarifications and Implications." *Health Affairs* (November/December 2004) 23:6, 181–191.

2. For a discussion of emerging private commercial roles see S. Raymond, *Enabling the Progress of the Mind: The Future of Philanthropy and Higher Education in America* (New York: Changing Our World, Inc., 2008), 38–39.

3. "The Chronicle Index of For-Profit Higher Education." *The Chronicle of Higher Education* (August 17, 2007), A25.

4. R. J. Yetman. "Tax-Motivated Expense Allocations by Nonprofit Organizations." *Accounting Review* (July 2001), 76:3, 297.

5. Internal Revenue Service, "Nonprofit Charitable Organization and Domestic Private Foundation Information Returns, and Exempt Organization Business Income Tax Returns: Elected Financial Data," 1985–2005. Table 16.

6. M. Riley. "Unrelated Business Income Tax Returns, 2000, With a Decade in Review, 1991–2000." *Statistics of Income Bulletin* (Spring 2004), 23:4, 135

7. S. Strom. "Tax Exemptions of Charities Face New Challenges." *New York Times*, May 26, 2008, A1.

8. Ibid.

9. S. Qualters, "IRS Takes a Closer Look at Universities." *National Law Journal* (October 20, 2008), 1.

10. S. Raymond. "The Impossibility of Boundaries: Globalization of Environmental Philanthropy." In S. Raymond, *Can Philanthropy Save the Planet? A Briefing on the Impact of Philanthropy on the Environment.* (New York: Changing Our World, Inc., 2008), 40.

11. Ibid., 41.

12. S. Raymond, *Enabling the Progress of the Mind: The Future of Philanthropy and Higher Education in America* (New York: Changing Our World, Inc., 2008), 46.

13. J. Lampman. "Donors Warm Up to Online Giving." *Christian Science Monitor*, June 23, 2008.

14. "The Wired Wealthy: Using the Internet to Connect with Your Middle and Major Donors." *Convio, Sea Change Strategies and Edge Research*, March 14, 2008.

15. S. Strom, "Study Shows First-Time Online Donors Often Do Not Return." *New York Times*, March 18, 2009, A13.

16. For a full and authoritative treatment of the phenomenon of social networking and its philanthropic implications, see T. Watson, *Cause Wired* (New York: John Wiley & Sons, 2008).

17. "Social Networking Growth." *Inside Facebook*, August 12, 2008. www.inside facebook.com/2008/08/12.

18. Ellison Research, February 2008; Institute for Social Research, January 2005; Wirthlin Worldwide, January 2003; Harris Interactive, 2003.

19. M. Richtel. "A Google Whiz Searches for His Place on Earth. Remade in America: The Newest Immigrants and Their Impact." *New York Times*, April 12, 2009, 1.

20. "Wealth in America 2008: Findings from a Survey of Millionaire Households." *Northern Trust*, January 2008, 35.

21. "College Students Helping America." Corporation for National and Community Service, October 2006, 6.

22. "Newsmakers: Anne Heald: Engaging Donors in New Ways to Promote Philanthropy." *Philanthropy News Digest*, November 19, 2003. www.foundationcenter. org/pnd/newsmakers.

23. S. McGee, "Next-Gen Givers." *Barrons*, December 1, 2008.

24. S. Raymond, B. Love, J. Moore. *Giving Through the Generations: Demanding Impact, Building Unity, Securing Legacy* (London: Campden Media, 2009).

25. K. Fulton and A. Blau, "Cultivating Change in Philanthropy." Monitor Company Group, 2005. 10.

26. "Study of High Net-Worth Philanthropy." Bank of America, 2008.

27. C. Preston. "Long Hours, Low Pay Turn Off Young Nonprofit Workers, Study Finds." *Chronicle of Philanthropy*, March 13, 2007, 5.

28. P. Rooney et al. *American Express Charitable Gift Survey, 2007* (Indianapolis, IN: Center on Philanthropy).

CHAPTER 5

Institutions Blaze New Trails
Innovations in Philanthropic Financial Support Strategies

He was a private citizen who sought no distinction of rank or title...
Rev. Newman Hall eulogy of George Peabody

His was a warfare against want.
Upon Peabody's temporary internment at Westminster Abbey, 1869

Nearly a century and a half ago, in 1867, the first modern foundation in the United States opened its doors. George Peabody, who began as an apprentice to a grocer and ended up as one of the wealthiest financiers of his time, capped a life of individual giving (the mode of philanthropy at the time) with the creation of the Peabody Fund, under a Board of Trustees, which administered grant making to establish open educational systems in the post–Civil War southern states. Peabody's reliance on independent administration of grant making set the stage for what would ultimately be the rise of billions of dollars of professional philanthropy in the United States.

Thematic Summary

Nonprofits cannot trigger complex strategies to reach complex resources from positions of economic panic. Taking advantage of philanthropic innovation requires constant, disciplined planning and monitoring. If capitalizing on philanthropic innovation is the "when all else fails" Plan B to a failed Plan A, then there is no Plan B.

Traditional Foundation Giving

From that initial organizational innovation has grown a philanthropic sector of more than 75,000 foundations,[1] annually distributing nearly $46 billion in funding for grants. The growth in the foundation sector has been particularly striking over the last decade, with a nearly 50 percent growth in the number of foundations in the country. Inflation-adjusted foundation giving has more than doubled. About 30,000 new foundations have been created in the last decade alone, an amazing 250 per month, or more than 10 every business day. If the number of foundations grows only at the median rate of growth of the last 15 years, there will be more than 110,000 foundations by 2015. Reflecting the extraordinary youthfulness of this philanthropic subsector, at that rate of growth, nearly 80 percent of foundations in the United States will have been formed just since 1980.[2]

The foundation sector is dominated by private independent foundations that, as shown in Exhibit 5.1, represent nearly 90 percent of grant-making institutions and more than 70 percent of foundation giving. There is, of course, tremendous concentration in the independent private foundation subsector.

Still, there remains striking concentration in the independent foundation sector, both geographically and financially. The five states with the largest number of foundations (New York, California, Texas, Florida, and Illinois, in that order) account for 40 percent of all private foundations and 45 percent of all foundation assets.[3] New York and California alone account for

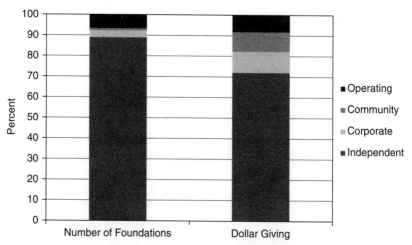

EXHIBIT 5.1 Distribution of Foundations and Giving by Type, 2006
Source: Foundation Center, 2008.

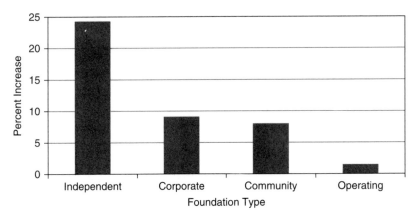

EXHIBIT 5.2 Percent Increase in Foundation Gifts Received, 2005–2006
Source: Foundation Center, 2008.

23 percent of all of the nation's foundations. Moreover, finances are also concentrated, this time by organization size not necessarily geography. The 25 largest foundations (a mere 0.03 percent of the institutional total) account for 20 percent of all foundation giving and 25 percent of assets.[4] For many nonprofits located outside the geographic concentration and unable to get the attention of large foundations, the proliferation of private foundations has not necessarily meant increased resource access.

The growth of foundation giving has come largely from new gifts, not from the appreciation of assets. In the 2005 to 2006 period, the value of assets in all types of foundations grew between 10 percent and 12 percent, but, as shown in Exhibit 5.2, gifts to private independent foundations increased by nearly 25 percent.

Community foundations have been an exception to that rule, where asset growth has outpaced the receipt of new gifts. For many community foundations, this has reflected two trends. On the one hand, the globalization of the economy and of wealth has meant that identification with "community" has changed. Executives do not spend long periods of time in one place. They are in Cincinnati after 10 years in Moscow and are likely to spend the next 10 years in Sao Paulo. Their sense of place is spread globally. On the other hand, even those who live in a single place have a broader sense of identity. Real-time electronic communication makes the global local. Moreover, residential sprawl redefines the sense of place. Greater metropolitan Chicago, for example, is composed of 3,800 square miles, 265 different municipalities, 1,200 separate tax districts, and parts of six counties and three states. Even greater Birmingham, Alabama, is composed of 8 counties,

3 major cities, 23 smaller cities, and 99 individual neighborhoods, each with its own neighborhood association. What does "community" mean with such dispersion and sprawl?

For corporate foundations, the pattern of the last few years has been somewhat different from their private and community counterparts. Although giving has increased, the number of corporate foundations actually declined by 2.3 percent between 2006 and 2007, a loss of 59 foundations.[5] Some of this may be due to changes in corporate strategy, bringing giving inside the operational budget, and some may be due to mergers and acquisitions when foundations are consolidated. There are two central tendencies that increasingly govern traditional corporate grant making, both of which supersede changes in institutional numbers.

The first is alignment with corporate interests and expertise. Although companies continue to commit some funds to the general needs of the communities in which they operate, their larger concern is to concentrate their giving on problems that resonate with their own industrial expertise and their own brand. As Frederic de Narp, President and CEO of Cartier North America, remarked in the deepest darkness of the 2008–2009 recession,

> Cartier has held true to the belief that giving back to our communities and supporting charitable programs is an integral part of our philosophy. There has never been such an unstable moment. Therefore now, more than ever, it is important for corporations to step up. Executive leadership is essential, and it is important to have philanthropy aligned with strategy.[6]

This emphasis on alignment opens up significant opportunities for relevant nonprofits and creates the need for thoughtful positioning on the part of those whose work is now well-aligned.

The second tendency is concern with measurable impact, a subject also addressed in the previous discussion of Next-Gen philanthropy in Chapter 4, "Emerging Nonprofit Revenue Parameters." All foundations have recently begun to emphasize the impact of their grant making, but for corporate foundations the emphasis is central. A 2004 survey of foundation executives found that corporate foundations are more often deeply involved in grant implementation and consider impact to be a central concern. Nearly half (43 percent) of corporate foundations believed measurable outcomes were an important criteria for grant making, compared to 30 percent of independent foundations.[7]

The strategic implications of evolution in traditional foundation giving are several-fold. First, because the foundation sector is so young, it can also be extraordinarily innovative in its approach to resource allocation. We shall expand on this observation later in this chapter.

Second, the proliferation of foundations provides nonprofit revenue opportunity, but also equivalent management challenge. The result is a multiplicity of expectations about results and impacts, and expectations about documentation, for a relatively small grant amount. Indeed, the average foundation grant to a nonprofit is $25,000. It is managerially difficult, and often cost-prohibitive, for small nonprofits to satisfy such multiple demands involving small amounts of funding. Hence, the growth of the foundation sector does not necessarily translate into tactical opportunity for nonprofits to strengthen failing revenues by expanding their foundation reach, even though the numbers of foundations have increased. Moreover, the time spent on satisfying multiple foundations' reporting demands can be especially costly in times of economic crisis when every (scarce) dollar is consumed by service provision. Foundation proliferation can be a management problem as much as a funding opportunity.

Third, although many "community" nonprofits can clearly define their geographic service areas and can clearly define community, the problems of definition facing community foundations means that those developing funds at community foundations may not, in fact, define "community" in a way that aligns with service nonprofits. Again, the appearance of growth may not match the realities of nonprofit service areas or financial needs.

In sum, the growth of the foundation sector in the United States does not always map well onto the revenue needs of nonprofits facing financial crisis in a failing economy. Revenue strategies that include foundation tactics, therefore, will not be easily generalized across nonprofit types or service area geography.

Moreover, and in part because of proliferation, there is increasing interest among traditional foundations in finding ways to collaborate in their work, and thereby incentivize nonprofits to collaborate. The recognition that extremely complex problems require a critical mass of resources, which is beyond the capacity of most foundations, has led to innovations in foundation co-funding. Organizations like the Bravewell Collaborative and Foundations for a Better Oregon are examples of this trend. Future nonprofit strategy will need to take into account the degree to which this type of collaboration on the part of funders will be expected on the part of nonprofits as well.

New Strategies for Supporting Societal Missions

But those problems are, in some way, the least of the complexity. Foundations themselves are rethinking how they use the totality of their resources on the societal commons to address needs. Foundations control about $600 billion of investable resources. Increasingly, even innovations in

Philanthropic Collaboration Leads to Economic Development: The Case of Action Greensboro

For most of the twentieth century, the economy of Greensboro, North Carolina, our home, thrived along with its profitable industries: textiles, furniture, and tobacco. In the mid-1990s, the situation changed suddenly and dramatically, however, as manufacturing began moving offshore and more and more jobs began to be outsourced. In 2001, when local elected officials had not acknowledged the urgency of making economic development a top priority, Greensboro foundation leaders began meeting to develop strategies to revive the city's economy. In 2002, our Foundation, Toleo, joined five other foundations in this effort, called Action Greensboro. To establish the organization's priorities, groups of citizens were invited to visit comparable cities and task forces of volunteers worked with corporate and higher education leaders. Funded by the foundations, corporations, and individuals, Action Greensboro initially raised $35 million. This initial funding, spent on public education, entrepreneurial initiatives, downtown revitalization, attraction of young professionals, and community branding, leveraged $100 million in additional private investment by 2005. Among the fruits of Action Greensboro's efforts are a new downtown baseball park, a center city park, a new building for the county's health and social service agencies, and increased partnership between the business community and local colleges and universities. In April 2007, the foundations' collaboration in establishing and guiding Action Greensboro was awarded the Council on Foundations' inaugural Distinguished Grantmaker Award.

Two additional foundations joined Action Greensboro's leadership in 2008. The executive directors continue to meet once a week, as they have since 2001, to ensure that their vision remains shared and focused and that, as new opportunities present themselves, they can be quickly seized to continue the city's economic momentum.

Leonard and Tobee Kaplan
Founders
Cathy Levinson
Executive Director
The Toleo Foundation

traditional grant making are becoming only a portion of how foundations move resources into the nonprofit sector. Robust strategies for relating to foundation funding will increasingly require innovation on the part of nonprofit revenue structure and management.

There are several key areas of innovation, some of which have implications for nonprofit revenue strategies and some of which do not. For example, although only a small minority of foundations engage in the practice, proxy voting represents a strategy for linking assets to mission.[8] For foundations such as the Nathan E. Cummings Foundation, using the shareholder proxy for equities held in their endowment allows the foundation to bring its social concerns to the table of corporations in which its assets are invested. Proxy voting is also, of course, used by large nonprofit organizations to pursue their missions. When the assets of universities, hospitals, and even nonprofit pension funds are included, nonprofits hold well over $5 trillion in assets.[9] This is a not-inconsequential voice on the social commons. Strategies such as proxy voting allow nongrant resources to be aligned with foundation (and nonprofit) mission, but they do not necessarily impact nonprofit revenues.

However, at least four innovations in the use of philanthropic resources do provide opportunities (and challenges) for nonprofit finance. All share in common an effort to link philanthropic resources to markets in ways that leverage the capacity and impact of philanthropy itself.

Mission-Related Investing

Mission-related investing (MRI) is the process of using foundation assets to contribute to the success of organizations serving the societal mission to which the foundation is committed. This "all of resources" approach attempts to turn the corpus of foundation funds into a mission-directed tool, just as grants are used to strengthen mission-relevant nonprofits. Mission-related investing (and program-related investing described below) has been pursued since the mid-1960s, enabled by Section 4944 of the Tax Reform Act of 1969, which allowed investing that advanced charitable objectives to be counted as charitable activity. However, as illustrated in Exhibit 5.3, real growth has come only in the last decade. Today, about 100 foundations pursue MRI. They are of all types and sizes, including corporate and community foundations. About 30 percent of those using MRI strategies have less than $50 million in assets, indicating perhaps that smaller foundations see MRI as a mechanism for expanding the reach of their resources even while preserving the long-term stability of their assets. Rather than eroding assets by grant making in excess of the 5 percent outflow requirement of the IRS, smaller foundations compensate for their overall financial size by deploying their assets. With larger grant-making capacity, larger foundations may not see equivalent benefits relative to mission.

Over time, the resource flow is not insignificant. Between 2001 and 2005, foundations committed nearly $890 million to 520 deals through mission

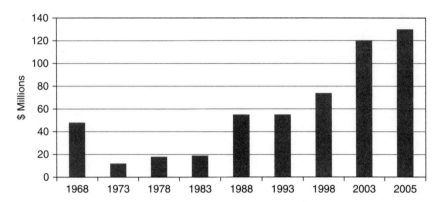

EXHIBIT 5.3 Annual Dollar Value of New Committed Mission Investments by Foundation, 1968–2005

Source: FSG Social Impact Advisors, 2007.

investments. Although the dollar commitment is nearly equally divided between debt and equity asset classes, the majority of deals have been through loan arrangements as noted in Exhibit 5.4. The vast majority of mission-related investments are in housing, economic development, education, and the environment. These four areas account for 85 percent of MRI deals but less than 50 percent of the value of resources allocated to foundation grants.[10]

Although more common in such areas as the environment, mission-related investing has also been applied to areas of poverty alleviation. MRI has been allocated to microfinance institutions, for example, to bolster the small lending operations to the impoverished by using investment capital

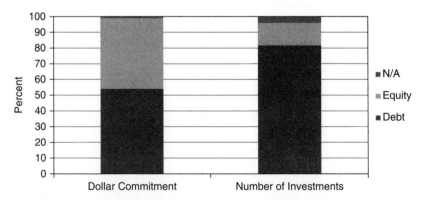

EXHIBIT 5.4 Mission Investment by Asset Class, 2001–2005

Source: FSG Social Impact Advisors, 2007.

from foundations rather than pure grant making.[11] As experience builds and interest grows, it is likely that foundations will look for new ways to flow the investment of their assets into markets that serve their missions.

Yet the effort remains well below foundation capacity. Only about $130 million in annual investment is taking place on an estimated total capital corpus in the foundation community of more than half a trillion dollars. Certainly one of the major impediments is concern over asset returns. Most foundations are created in perpetuity; that is, boards of directors are responsible, in part, for seeing that assets produce long-term financial stability. The perception that MRI does not result in market-comparable returns creates concerns over whether MRI, however much it serves programmatic mission, will not serve the asset mission of preservation and growth.

In addition to using their capital base for market investments that power markets into the societal commons, foundations are developing, or expanding, new ways of relating to nonprofits other than through grant making. These strategies reach into traditional nonprofit organizations, but encourage them to think about themselves and their community in different ways.

Program-Related Investing

Although similar to mission-related investing,[12] program-related investments (PRI) focus more specifically on nonprofits. MRIs deploy resources to both for-profit and nonprofit entities engaged in market activities; PRIs are used to leverage philanthropic capital with other sources of capital, reduce nonprofit costs of capital for expansion, create nonprofit financing sustainability, and/or enable large distributions of capital at a particular period of time necessary for a foundation to meet the 5 percent distribution rule yet ensure that the capital is paid back over time.

With the average foundation grant hovering around $25,000 and the average grant of even the largest foundations only slightly more than $200,000 (Exhibit 5.5), it has become clear to some philanthropies that grant making will never get many nonprofits to a point of sustainable financing. What is often needed is to enable nonprofits to access or build capital, not simply to hold the line on this year's operating budget. So PRI strategies use a variety of methods to bolster finances, especially where nonprofits are engaged in marketlike endeavors. PRI mechanisms include loans, cash equivalent deposits (to development banks or credit unions), equity (in projects with a direct charitable purpose), and loan guarantees. The targets of the strategy are either individual nonprofits or nonprofit intermediaries within communities, who aggregate such resources and redistribute them to community programs in ways that flow large amounts of resources to significant problems in disciplined financial ways. A classic example of the strategy is the Boston Community Loan Fund (BCLF), which aggregates PRIs from

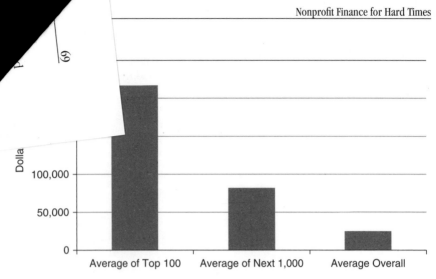

EXHIBIT 5.5 Average Size of Foundation Grant by Size of Foundation
Source: Foundation Center.

Selling the Vision: The Voice of Social Enterprise

Our attraction to social enterprise is natural. We're captivated by visionaries whose unbelievable vigor for justice and ingenuity has created magnificent social changes. For us Millennials, it is a field inundated with wild optimism, purpose, and inspiration. The biggest motivator for our career changes from sommelier and banker, respectively, was the same as that of many entrepreneurs: We think our idea can change the world.

Actually, we didn't know that we were involved in a social enterprise until someone told us. We only understood three things. First, reducing poverty in Africa requires creating opportunity. Second, our product has unique value as a messaging and fund-raising tool. Third, we were reluctant to leave the success of our venture in the hands of grant makers or a few generous wealthy individuals. (This was an especially uncomfortable notion for the banker.) So we began to explore the ways to link the wine industry, historically and traditionally closed to Africans, to economic opportunity by developing a nonprofit vineyard in South Africa to provide industrial experience and entry for black South Africans.

The International Society of Africans in Wine (ISAW) was founded to use wine as a way to reduce poverty. Our mission reads, *Building sustainable communities through viticulture*. We intentionally developed a curious and provocative mission and acronym, which became our point of engagement. This was the first thing we did right. Ironically, the first thing we did wrong was trying to explain what we did.

The story of the South African wine industry is deep and dark. Wine in South Africa is intrinsically linked to slavery, segregation, oppression, and social disparity. What today is a $3 billion annual industry began in 1652 after the Dutch colonized Table Bay, and later planted vines with slave labor. The fact that wine is produced in Africa is a revelation to most Americans, and its history is unknown, or at best unspoken. For fear of being perceived as more social club than enterprise, we started to validate our charity by telling this dark story. It was too much. When told in its entirety, few would argue that centuries of institutionalized oppression would not adversely affect the disenfranchised class. But who has time to tell (or listen) to the "entire story"? We had an amazing messenger (wine) sending the wrong message.

Instead, we started to let our products talk. When someone says "I love this wine" their enthusiasm redoubles when they learn that they are supporting the only black family-owned winery in Africa. We've learned that focusing on outcomes rather than origins is a more compelling way to communicate weighty and complex social issues. We've now gotten it down to a four-word tagline: "Drink Well, Do Good." This is a concept that everyone can understand and embrace.

True, this is more marketing than social enterprise, but that is our point. Nonprofits looking to shift into social enterprise become flustered when they "don't have a product to sell." Until recently, we didn't either. Nonprofits should focus on mission and message first, product second. It may be that your product is a clearly articulated message. As giving grows more competitive, expanding your visibility and audience may have the same desired return as a "tangible" product offering. Our biggest successes came only after exploring social enterprise beyond the context of just selling a product.

Learning to shift our communications to a direct and succinct message has allowed more effective interpretation and engagement. As you're developing a product to sell, remember the real magic is in thinking more enterprise-like; messages too can be sold.

Stephen Satterfield
Co-Founder
P. J. Bullock
Co-Founder
ISAW

foundations and individuals and uses them to lend not just for affordable housing and day-care institutions, but also for environmental preservation and community social services. Indeed, in one of the first PRIs, the Cleveland Foundation provided a PRI to buy and restore several historic theaters in downtown Cleveland.[13] The resources can be significant. Since its founding in 1985, the BCLF has provided more than $100 million in loans to more than 200 local nonprofits.[14]

Program-related investments are also increasingly used by individual philanthropists working through social enterprise funds or donor-advised funds (DAF). The philanthropist opens a fund in a DAF, which then makes a program-related investment in the relevant nonprofit. The DAF manages the due diligence and repayments process for the philanthropist for a fee. The philanthropist is able to support a nonprofit yet create a long-term philanthropic corpus; the nonprofit gets, at a minimum, below-market rate access to capital; the DAF earns a fee for its loan management role. The advantage to the nonprofit often extends beyond the PRI itself because access to those funds can enable the nonprofit to leverage more significant lending in the commercial sector and/or attract larger numbers of traditional philanthropic gifts on the basis of a significant expression of confidence by the provider of the PRI.

It should be noted that the DAF-based resources are particularly difficult to include in nonprofit revenue strategy. In most such funds, especially those that are commercial, the donor remains anonymous and his or her substantive priorities are not public. The DAF at Fidelity Investments, for example, is the nation's largest charity in terms of assets. Other investment funds also manage DAFs, with the total funds base of each being more than $1 billion.[15] These are the accumulated philanthropic intentions of thousands of individual investors, but the identity of the investors, their giving history, and their preferences are all unknown. It is difficult to plan for a DAF-based revenue stream, therefore, and the cultivation tools normally used by a nonprofit to develop a personal relationship with a donor are also blunted. There is something of a lottery characteristic to the DAF element. The nonprofit may research the DAF and submit proposals, but, like the lottery, the wise nonprofit does not plan on paying next month's mortgage with the winnings.

PRIs do not fit every need or every mission of every nonprofit. But they are gaining growing interest on the part of foundations that seek to move larger amounts of capital to problem solving in ways that can be repaid and thus preserve the financial base of the foundation itself.

Social Enterprise Support

In a speech to family foundations in 2006, AOL founder and philanthropist Steve Case remarked, "There's no logical reason why the private sector and the social sector should operate on separate levels, where one is about making money and the other about serving society. I believe we can and should be integrating these missions."[16]

Case has found himself increasingly among a range of like-minded philanthropic leaders. There is a growing recognition among foundations that even grants can contribute to nonprofit stability if they encourage nonprofits to think and act like entrepreneurs. "Social enterprise" takes on many meanings and now comes in many forms. But its central characteristics are:[17]

- *Market orientation.* They produce goods or services that meet the needs of a market and operate with financial discipline as would any commercial business.
- *Social aims.* They are explicitly organized to meet a social need, and their profits/surpluses are reinvested to achieve that objective.
- *Social ownership.* Most are organized by social groups or nonprofits and are accountable to the wider community or their stakeholders.

Social enterprises may be for-profit institutions, freestanding nonprofits, or market-oriented elements of traditional nonprofits. In all their forms, they use markets to generate revenues that serve their larger social missions. Institutions like Juma Ventures operate businesses to provide job training and opportunities to disadvantaged youth. Fair trade organizations gather and market the coffee of small growers who would not otherwise be able to reach international markets. Social enterprise organic bakeries produce goods for local markets, pursue environmental missions, and train and employ disadvantaged workers.

There is some evidence that social enterprise funding withstands economic downturns. Indeed, in the 2007 to 2009 downturn, strengthening Community Development Financial Institutions was actually part of the economic stimulus package passed by Congress to restart the economy.[18]

The examples, permutations, and combinations are many, and the literature is increasing rich.[19] The point here is that traditional foundation philanthropy is increasingly interested in seeing nonprofit organizations develop market-melded strategies that are consistent with mission but also provide the prospect for revenue diversity. Taking the mission to the market is, therefore, an important component of developing multipronged nonprofit strategies for aligning with the changing interests of foundations and philanthropists.

Harnessing Investing to Philanthropy

Another innovation is the marrying of investment to philanthropy. The variations on this innovation are many. Two examples make the point that new strategies to flow resources to nonprofit needs are emerging that are deeply tied to financial management and investment strategies. They both broaden potential resource pools and may make those pools extremely problematic in times of economic stress, particularly stress that is rooted deeply in capital markets themselves.

The Children's Investment Fund Foundation was created by British financier Chris Hohn and his wife, Jamie, to aid children in the developing world. The foundation is not simply funded by Hohn himself, but it is built into his investment strategy for his clients as well. The Hohns' hedge fund and the Children's Investment Fund (TCI) are linked to their charity, the Children's Investment Fund Foundation. TCI funds the foundation in two ways. TCI gives 0.5 percent of funds under management (effectively a third of its annual fee) to the foundation. In addition, however, investors in TCI pay an extra 0.5 percent fee to the foundation if TCI produces returns above 11 percent per year.[20] Obviously, in down markets, that extra does not materialize. But, over time, resources do accumulate. It is market success that fuels philanthropic growth. Just as Steve Case has noted, the two do not represent necessarily distinct genotypes.

RSF Social Finance provides another example of the emerging dimensions of social finance as well as the evolutionary growth of traditional foundations. Founded in 1936 as the Rudolf Steiner Foundation, RSF engaged in traditional grant making for nearly 50 years. In 1984, it reinvented itself as RSF Social Finance and is now an investment fund and a donor-advised fund. It attracts capital from socially conscious investors who wish to see their capital deployed, with a return on investment but for purposes of economic opportunity at the community level. RSF invests (in the traditional sense of the word) in sustainable food and agriculture, education and the arts, and ecological stewardship. It also is host to a donor-advised fund, through which investors make philanthropic grants to social enterprises. It has more than 1,000 clients, $120 million in assets, more than $50 million in loans outstanding, and 94 donor-advised funds.[21]

Cause-Related Marketing

Innovation in linking philanthropy to markets also increasingly characterizes corporate social engagement. Rather than simply writing checks to nonprofits, corporations are linking their brands to a cause in the marketplace, harnessing giving to consumer behavior. The resources for these cause-related marketing (CRM) and sponsorship strategies do not rest in the budgets of corporate giving programs or corporate foundations. They are part of marketing strategies, so there is little concrete information on the dollar value of corporate investments in this area. The best guess is that

Challenging Models to Create New Opportunities

There is only so much money that flows from nonprofits and government each year to address major international health issues.

In hard times, that money inevitably shrinks. As new issues arise, these limited dollars get stretched across more projects.

When (RED) began, we decided not to play for a share of the existing dollars directed to fight AIDS in Africa. We asked, "How do we grow the pie overall and create more money to help pay for AIDS treatment?"

Our answer took us right to the billions of dollars that change hands each day between companies that create desirable products and the consumers who want them. Could we really redirect a portion of these transactions to buy AIDS medicine for people dying thousands of miles away?

Turns out, yes, we could.

That is, if we were willing to challenge the principles of traditional philanthropy and, instead, play by the rules of business. Although philanthropy is often driven from a beautiful selflessness, business is quite the opposite. At the core of capitalism, the company operates to maximize its return on investment.

(RED) had to make doing good, good business.

When a shopper buys a (RED) product, they get something they want or need and the company makes a profit. (RED) corporate partners secure new customers and shift their brand perception and people living with AIDS in Africa get the pills they need to stay alive.

So did we grow the pie with this approach? Does doing good make for good business? Yes.

Before (RED) was created, businesses had given just $5 million to the Global Fund to Fight AIDS, Tuberculosis, and Malaria over four years. Since (RED) launched in 2006, our programs have generated more than $130 million for the Global Fund—100 percent of which is directed to fund AIDS programs in Africa.

Susan Smith Ellis
Chief Executive Officer
(RED)

CRM expenditures totaled $1.52 billion in 2008, a figure that was 86 percent higher than in 2002 (Exhibit 5.6).[22]

As Americans, indeed as global markets, become more connected and issue conscious, the corporate interest in these types of strategies is

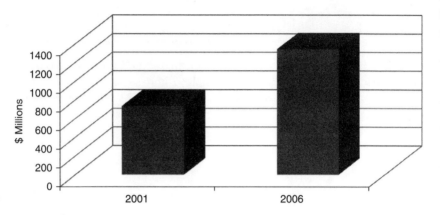

EXHIBIT 5.6 Cause-Related Marketing Expenditures, 2002 and 2008

Source: IEG Inc.

increasing. In one survey, nearly 90 percent of consumers said they would change brands if a brand was aligned with a good cause.[23] A 2008 Cone, Inc. study with Duke's Fuqua School of Business found that linking products to causes can increase sales by as much as 74 percent.[24] Indeed, research on "green" issues finds that nearly three-quarters of shoppers purchase environmentally friendly products and over half make a special effort to patronize retailers with "green" reputations.[25]

This is not to say that all nonprofits can benefit from CRM strategies, or even that all that could are likely to benefit. Corporations engage with nonprofits and causes that align with their market interests. This is a logical consequence of resources being allocated from marketing budgets. In challenging economic times, however, finding mechanisms for linking nonprofit effort to the societal commons that benefits both a nonprofit mission and the needs of private commerce may be particularly attractive. Such strategies strengthen nonprofits, establish networks of consumers whose interests can be converted to philanthropic relationships, and contribute to the viability of companies whose presence in communities is important for a spectrum of reasons from employment to the community tax base. Such "win-win" strategies may be particularly attractive to companies when competition in a shrinking economy becomes ever more heated.

For the nonprofit, however, strategy is key. Corporations have no lack of opportunities to spend their marketing dollars. The nonprofit must understand that the competition for those dollars is as real as the competition for the corporate philanthropic dollar.

Chapters 8 and 9 of this book will speak to the specifics of strategies for assessing the viability of CRM revenue options for nonprofits, large and small. In general, the mission and reach of the nonprofit must align with the target business's focus. In many ways, a CRM relationship is not a "gift" from a corporation; it is a corporate investment in a nonprofit cause that promises to bring both societal gain and market advantage. Moreover, scale must be sufficient; a few people interested in an obscure problem are seldom a "market" of adequate size to compete for market-driven CRM dollars. Collaboration among a range of nonprofits may be essential to make the CRM option real, and assessing the costs and benefits of such collaboration must be part of revenue strategy.

Capitalizing on Innovation: The Prerequisite of Planning

All of these innovations in the way that dollars are flowing to the societal commons can benefit nonprofits in both good and bad economic times. They are, however, complex. They require considerable research, thought, and strategy. They also require skills that may not be present in the day-to-day operations of many nonprofits, and so require developing leadership (including volunteers) capable of assessing the revenue attractiveness of innovative funding and ensuring its alignment with mission.

Thoughts about the robustness of innovation are unlikely to be helpful if they are relegated to the shelf, if they are seen as Plan B, the "if all else fails" fall-back to declining contributions from the usual, traditional sources. If capitalizing on innovation is Plan B, then there is no Plan B. Nonprofits cannot trigger complex strategies to reach complex resources from positions of panic. Detailed research and planning are essential. That planning must be done as a fundamental part of nonprofit revenue strategy, and mechanisms for identifying new innovations must constantly bring those opportunities to revenue planning for vetting and consideration. Capitalizing on innovation cannot be spontaneous. Planning and execution must be disciplined and constantly monitored and appropriately adjusted.

Innovations in philanthropic flows will only increase in the future. Broad commitment to social problem solving of a new generation of philanthropic and corporate leaders—many of whom have created whole new industries, whole new technologies, whole new ways of living and communicating and who, therefore, see change not as episodic but as life's constant. In the coming decade, innovation on the part of philanthropy will need to be met with flexibility and creativity on the part of the nonprofit. The successful nonprofit—seeking revenue strategies that will withstand economic turmoil—will need to have the ability to understand, to adjust to, and to capitalize on these innovations as a matter of its central management competency and responsibility.

Notes

1. This estimate is from Foundation Growth and Giving Estimates, Current Outlook 2009 Edition, Washington, DC: The Foundation Center, 1. Data from the Internal Revenue Service differ markedly, indicating that there are more than 112,000 foundations in the nation, of which 84,000 are of sufficient size to file a tax return. However, deeper sector analysis based on the IRS number is not possible because the IRS does not aggregate other indicators, such as grantmaking details.
2. Calculated by Changing our World, Inc., based on time series data from the National Center for Charitable Statistics.
3. Center for Charitable Statistics, 2008.
4. Foundation Growth and Giving Estimates, 2008. Washington, DC: The Foundation Center, 2008. 10–12.
5. Ibid., 4.
6. E. Anderson, "CEOs Encourage Corporate Philanthropy in Trying Times." February 26, 2009. www.onphilanthropy.com.
7. F. Ostrower, *Attitudes and Practices Concerning Effective Philanthropy: Survey Report* (Washington, DC: The Urban Institute Center on Nonprofits and Philanthropy, 2004), 6.
8. The Ostrower Survey indicates that proxy voting is more common among foundations with international interests than among those with purely domestic grantmaking. Ibid., 38.
9. "A Call for Mission-Based Investing by America's Private Foundations," National Committee on Responsive Philanthropy, September 2005.
10. S. Cooch and M. Kramer. "Compounding Impact: Mission Investing by U.S. Foundations." FSG Social Impact Advisors, March 2007, 29.
11. See extensive examples in "Mission Possible: Emerging Opportunities for Mission-Connected Investment," New Economics Foundation, London, 2008.
12. The two terms are often used interchangeably. In this work, however, MRI relates to investment in market-quality asset classes such that societal missions are aligned with markets for purposes of growing foundation assets consistent with mission. PRI refers to the use of foundation resources to provide capital to nonprofits at levels or for growth that might not be possible with grantmaking because the capital provided will be repaid.
13. "Reframing Endowment as a Tool for Community Leadership," *Future Matters*, Monitor Institute (Spring 2007).
14. "Investing in Your Mission," *Family Giving News* 4:3 (March 2004).
15. P. Brest and H. Harvey, *Money Well Spent* (New York: Bloomberg Press, 2008), 244.
16. S. Case, "The Future of Foundations: Blending Business and Philanthropy." Speech given to the Family Foundations Conference, Honolulu, Hawaii, January 30, 2006.

17. Derived from the Social Enterprise Coalition.

18. R. Hacke, "As the Economic Crisis Deepens, Socially Oriented Capital Emerges." www.onPhilanthropy.com, March 5, 2009.

19. See, for example, S. M. Oster, C. W. Massarsky, and C. L. Beinhacker (eds.), *Generating and Sustaining Nonprofit Earned Income: A Guide to Successful Enterprise Strategies* (New York: John Wiley & Sons, 2004).

20. J. MacKintosh, "TCI Founder Hohn Gives £230 Million to His Charitable Organization." *Financial Times of London*, July 2, 2007, 1.

21. RSF Social Finance Fact Sheet, as of January 2009.

22. IEG Sponsorship Report 2009.

23. *2007 Cone Cause Evolution and Environmental Survey.* (Boston: Cone and Company, 2007), 7.

24. S. Mahoney, "Cause-Related Marketing Generates Double Digit Sales Gains." *Media Post News and Marketing Daily*, October 7, 2008, 1.

25. 2007 Annual National Shopping Behavior Survey. KPMG LLP, 2008.

Does the Economy Matter?

The Complexity of Economic Cycles and Nonprofit Revenues

Frugality is good, if liberality be joined with it. The first is leaving off superfluous expenses; the last bestowing them to the benefit of those in need. The first without the last begets covetousness; the last without the first begets prodigality.

William Penn, *Some Fruits of Solitude*

One must now ask whether, and if so how, trends in the larger economy matter to nonprofits, after having examined the increasing complexity of philanthropic giving strategies and of nonprofit revenue structure. The question is not as simple as it may seem.

Thematic Summary

For nonprofits, economic cycles are often not seen as opportunities for change and adaptation, but rather as threats to mission. The analysis of economic change, therefore, is often premised on the negative (does it hurt) rather than on the positive (does it help) the nonprofit sector. The answer to the "hurt" part of the question is "sometimes." The answer to the "help" part of the question is "it should, but it usually doesn't because of failed vision." Economic change represents an opportunity for nonprofits to reexamine programs and strategies and adjust to further take advantage of a renewed economy. However, this requires that nonprofits see their missions as sails, not anchors, when the winds of change blow.

The Opportunity of Cycles

Any open economy is cyclical, with periods of expansion and periods of contraction. Indeed, cyclicality is a strength. What gives an economy the opportunity for long-term stable growth is its ability to turn failure to its advantage, to turn old investments into new approaches to markets. Economies stumble for all manner of reasons. Markets change and businesses fail to adapt. New technologies emerge and painfully replace old ways. Public policies fall short of adjusting to changing capital structures. Politics gets in the way of rational economic behavior. The list is long. The advantage of change is that capital can then be redeployed. Both financial capital and human resources shift from what does not work or what is past to what does work or what holds promise for the future. Rather than being trapped in old interests, or inefficiencies, or tottering failures, both money and skills can migrate to more productive efforts. Buggy whip manufacturing moves aside to make way for the two-stroke engine, which is replaced by the four-cylinder engine, which moves aside to make way for the hybrid engine. The loss of buggy whip jobs is painful but perhaps not regrettable in the long term.

Adam Smith's "invisible hand" of the market pushes the economy upward through the downward period of creative destruction. This does not make the downward portion of the cycle any less painful for those who endure it, of course, but the ultimate utility of the redeployment of economic capacity is undeniable.

Healthy economies are cyclic. This is also true for nonprofits. Jolts to the economic status quo represent opportunities to reexamine, realign, and renew organizations. Adjustment and innovation are, by definition, disorienting. All individuals are discomforted by change. Most organizations break out in hives at the thought. But the creative destruction of economic cycles produces long-term growth and resilience.

Nonprofits and Economic Change: Treating Mission as a Sail, Not an Anchor

For nonprofits, however, there are two consequential problems, however economically beneficial is cyclic change. The second in some ways is a direct result of the first.

First, there is no "invisible hand" in the nonprofit sector. There is no market. As noted previously in Chapter 3, "Philanthropy within Financial Structures," it is true that for some nonprofits (e.g., hospitals), service provision, in fact, takes place within a market. For many, however, supply and demand are not mediated by price (either the price of capital or the price of goods or services). Supply, demand, and price do not combine to spark innovation. So an economic downturn is not an opportunity to fold up the tent and move on to more productive endeavors. Between 30 percent and 50 percent of new businesses fail within the first five years of operation.[1] Failure is part of the consequences of changed environments or poor market analysis. For nonprofits, however, fidelity to mission often trumps a changed environment.

This is a central reason for the extreme discomfiture with which nonprofits view economic cycles. For most nonprofits, mission is the core, the central focus of their rationale for being. Mission becomes an anchor, holding the institution firm to its purposes. Existence begins with and fulfills mission. Economic cycles are not seen as opportunities for change and adaptation, but rather as threats to mission. But, viewed that way, mission is an anchor, tethering the nonprofit in place. Unable to adjust, the organization feels threatened by change, fearful the cycles will endanger its stability. Instead, mission can be seen as a sail, providing the capacity to gather in change and power the nonprofit forward.

Of course, a firm hand at a functioning tiller is also critical, a matter to be discussed in Chapter 8, "Common Principles for Robust Strategy." If mission is seen as a sail—that is, as a means for harnessing change to intended direction—rather than a way to stay in place, revenue strategies for harnessing the sail to the tiller become robust ways to move forward.

Second, and as a result, nonprofits often face economic cycles in crisis, seeking to hold fast long enough to "weather the storm" and return to their previous financial stability to provide a preexisting menu of goods and services on the societal commons. This is because most nonprofits do not constantly take the pulse of economic change. Healthy economies are never still. They are constantly innovating and adapting. Businesses are constantly dying and being created. Even in a growing economy, as many as half of all small businesses fail within the first five years of operation. Those failures are not easy for the founders, of course, but the economy overall expects such turnover and recycles labor into more productive or successful endeavors.

The nonprofit sector overall does not operate under this general expectation. Moreover, many nonprofits do not have mechanisms (nor do they see it as a priority) to constantly monitor the pulse of economic change. When the inevitable downturn comes, there is surprise, consternation, and panic. No sustainable strategy was ever developed in the midst of panic. The predisposition to monitor and anticipate change, and to plan ahead for it, is a critical prerequisite to developing revenue strategies for both mainsail and spinnaker that will fill a nonprofit's sails even when seas are stormy.

Of course, not all cycles are alike. Some cycles produce exciting gusts that send us skimming across the seas; some produce gale-force threats to the main mast. Deep recessions[2] hold much more destruction and much more pain than the economic norm, and the climb out is longer as human and financial capital struggle to adjust to produce renewed and higher economic growth. Between October 2007 and January 2009, the S&P 500 lost 48 percent of its market value. The federal budget deficit, projected to be $438 billion in September 2008, had ballooned to an anticipated $1.2 trillion by January 2009 and nearly $1.4 trillion four weeks later. The 2008–2009 recession can easily and accurately be cast as economic crisis.

For nonprofits, the question is whether economic cycles, especially recessions, are associated with revenue declines and, for purposes of this book, especially with declines in revenue from private contributions.

The Past Record of Private Contributions and the Economy

Private financial contributions to nonprofit organizations are part of U.S. culture. Even in the depression of the 1930s, while philanthropic giving declined initially, it doubled in inflation-adjusted terms between 1933 and 1941.[3] What does long-term data tell us? There are many ways to look at the correlation. Most analysts use two financial measures: (1) changes in GDP and (2) changes in the equity markets. Neither is particularly enlightening.

Over 40 years, private giving has represented between 1.7 percent and 2.2 percent of the economy, a changing amplitude of only half a percentage point. In that period, as noted in Exhibit 6.1, there have been only two points at which private giving has declined for more than a single year. The first was in the early 1970s and the last was in 2001–2003. In both cases, the

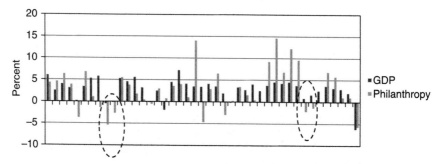

EXHIBIT 6.1 Year-over-Year Change in GDP Compared to Change in Giving, 1966–2008
Source: Giving USA and Bureau of Economic Analysis, Department of Commerce.

decline was for two consecutive years. The first was during the shocks of the oil embargo, the second was during the combination of the bursting of the technology bubble compounded by the terrorist attacks of September 11, 2001.

What is the possible message? It appears to take a shock to the economy of unprecedented proportions—a shock never before experienced—to derail American philanthropy for more than a single year. In the early to mid-1970s, it was the delinking of prices from the markets for a factor of economic production, in this case energy. In 2001–2003, the United States had experienced the greatest loss of life on U.S. soil since the Civil War. Whether history will prove that the 2008–2009 period reflects a similar experience is yet to be known. The 5.7 percent decline in giving in 2008 was significant. If accompanied by a drop in 2009, the historical pattern would hold—an unprecedented shock to the economy is needed to throw the culture of giving off its tracks.

By May 2009, with a 40 percent decline in the U.S. stock market, an economic recovery is not projected to begin until late 2009, and the near 10 percent unemployment is projected to remain above 6 percent until sometime in 2013. The likelihood that philanthropy would endure a two-year decline appears reasonable. The shock to the economy of plummeting housing values and disappearing financial assets represents a deep challenge to all sectors of the economy, including the nonprofit sector.

Even in periods of decline, however, philanthropy rebounds to levels higher than those experienced prior to or during the economic downturn. As illustrated in Exhibit 6.2, when the economy recovers, philanthropy recovers both quickly and at significant levels.

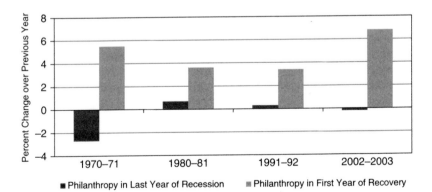

EXHIBIT 6.2 **Growth Record for Private Giving at Economic Recovery**
Source: Giving USA.

This is a critical point, and it deserves emphasis. It is why revenue strategy must anticipate and prepare for economic change. It is why nonprofits must plan for inevitable economic cycles and must remain proactive even in the depths of a downturn. Where an economic cycle results in philanthropic reductions, two elements are critical. First, revenue strategy must be diverse to counteract those reductions with other financial sources, many of which were discussed in previous chapters. Second, plans must be in place to take advantage of the inevitable strong upturn in philanthropy that follows the economic upturn. The organization that develops strategy after the fact of the economic upturn will find itself running hard to stay in the middle of the organizational pack. The race in the competitive nonprofit sector will go to the organizations poised to sprint in front of the strengthening economic winds.

If one looks at income behavior not in its macro measure (i.e., GDP) but in a micro measure (i.e., household expenditures) a similar picture of poor alignment emerges, as noted in Exhibit 6.3. Contributions as a portion of household expenditures do not move markedly in recessionary periods. Changing Our World examined detailed IRS household expenditure data from 1984 through 2007.[4] Contributions declined in the first year of a recessionary period and increased in the second. Furthermore, as a percentage of spending, contributions did not track recessions for any income group. Year-over-year changes were usually relatively small, and adjustments were present in and out of recessionary periods. The exception is the year-over-year change in contributions from the lowest quintile income groups, where shifts can be significant. Nevertheless, those shifts are not clearly tied to recession years, denoted by Exhibit 6.3 ovals.

The second traditional vector of analysis is to examine the relationship between philanthropy and the performance of the stock market. In part, this is probably because market slides can be so easily depicted and tend to be

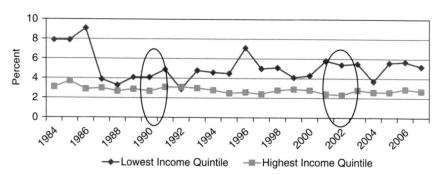

EXHIBIT 6.3   Cash Contributions as Percent of Income by Income Quintile, 1984–2007
Source: IRS.

a simple way to express economic times through popular media. The relevance of the measure for philanthropy, of course, is directly related to how people give. If giving is from assets, then assets may be a good measure of the propensity to give. If people give from income, however, then the relationship is probably weaker. True, the state of one's asset portfolio does affect the view of long-term income prospects. But it may not have equivalent dampening effects on short-term philanthropic behavior. This is especially true if a donor is giving to a nonprofit that has been a matter of historical support. The state of personal capital resources may not be a strong predictor of continued financial support in an economic downtrend. Loyalty and income capacity may combine to be more predictive than the state of a stock portfolio. Philanthropy that is deeply tied to personal commitments—what has been called "expressive philanthropy"—may persist even where total personal worth declines.

Before examining the evidence, perspective is important. Since 1995, the value of most mature stock portfolios has increased by 70 percent to 100 percent despite periodic market drops. In 1993, the Dow Jones Industrial Average reached a "record high" of 3,764. The Dow never closed over 6,000 until 1996. At the worst of its valuation in the 2008 to June 2009 period, the Dow dropped briefly to its 1997 levels of about 7,100. By June 2009, the market had gained back about 1,200 points, still a third less than its highest levels in 2007.

That having been said, huge declines in asset values are not accompanied by huge declines in philanthropy, at least not historically, as noted in Exhibit 6.4. If one looks at return on equities, the period 2000–2003 provides a marked illustration. In that period, return on equities plummeted. Although philanthropic giving also declined, it did not decline at anything compared

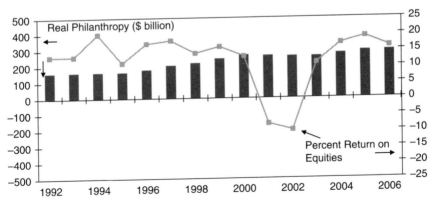

EXHIBIT 6.4 Inflation-Adjusted Philanthropy versus Return on Equities

Source: Giving USA and the Investment Company.

to the precipitous rates of equity. In other years, large changes, positive or negative, of return on equities did not track perfectly onto changes in philanthropic giving. The reason may be that, even for the wealthy, the vast majority of giving is out of income not out of assets. The 2008 surveys by Indiana University indicate that only a third of high-net-worth individuals gave or plan to give out of stocks or mutual funds, compared to more than 90 percent who gave or planned to give by cash or check.[5]

So, whether in terms of income or in terms of capital measures, predicting giving behavior based on gross economic measures is imperfect at best.

Disaggregating Data for Deeper Relationships

Disaggregating giving, however, and looking for surrogate measures does reveal better (but still not perfect) patterns. This requires that we look more deeply inside aggregated giving data and try to find patterns at a more detailed level that will provide insight on the economic linkage, and opportunity to predict giving behavior.

Individuals

More than 80 percent of philanthropy comes from individuals, the vast majority of that while they are alive. For individuals, giving is discretionary. That is, apart from religious dictates, for most individuals, giving is behavior that is financed at will from funds left over after basic needs (housing, food, education) have been met. Therefore, one wants to look for a measure that might affect individual behavior with discretionary funds. One could hypothesize that the relationship between giving and the economy is not at the level of macroeconomic measures like GDP but at the level of individual measures that enable (or impede) discretionary spending. Employment would certainly be one such measure.

As is seen in Exhibit 6.5, there is, in fact, a stronger correlation between increases in unemployment rates and decreases in individual giving. In general, when unemployment goes down, philanthropy goes up, and when unemployment goes up, philanthropy goes down. There are exceptions, but there are far fewer exceptions than with other macroeconomic indicators. If nonprofits wish to keep an eye on a single economic measure as a revenue Early Warning System, unemployment rates may provide the best guidance.

Work sponsored by the Bank of America at Indiana University[6] more deeply examined the behavior of wealthy individuals and found that, in times of financial crisis, they are likely to:

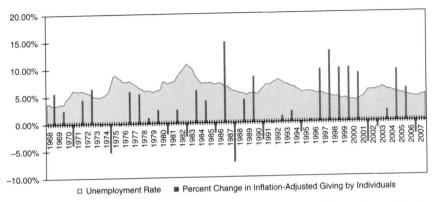

EXHIBIT 6.5 Change in Individual Giving Compared to Change in Unemployment Rate, 1968–2007

Source: Giving USA and Bureau of Economic Analysis, Department of Commerce.

- Favor nonprofits focused on basic human needs
- Significantly cut giving to nonprofits (by as much as 70 percent)
- But reduce their average giving by only 9.7 percent

Thus, while the wealthiest realign their substantive priorities markedly and reduce their giving, those reductions are relatively modest. Still, the reductions are in marked contrast to the expectation of the millennials, noted in Chapter 5, "Institutions Blaze New Trails," who intend to meet the market downturn with continued philanthropic commitment.

Foundations

Let us take another disaggregated example that illustrates the complexity of the relationship. Since most (but not all) foundations make grants from the investment earnings on their financial corpus, it is reasonable to expect that a financial downturn would be immediately felt by foundation grants. This would be doubly the case if foundations held to the legal requirement to distribute 5 percent of their assets to charity and did not show a propensity to distribute larger amounts in times of distress. What does the record show?

A near-term snapshot indicates that, in 2008, foundations increased their grant making. However, the extraordinary escalation in energy prices, which drove an inflation spike, meant that in real dollar terms, foundation giving held relatively steady. Nevertheless, during a short period of tremendous economic uncertainty, foundation giving did not show a marked decline.[7] Does that pattern hold over the longer term?

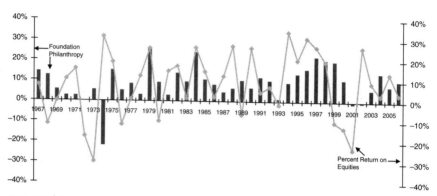

EXHIBIT 6.6 Annual Percentage Change: Foundation Philanthropy versus S&P 500
Source: Giving USA, and Robert Shiller.

Yes, but timing matters. There is about a one-year lag between changes in the Standard & Poor's 500 and changes in foundation philanthropy. The pattern is not perfect, but it is fairly consistent. As illustrated in Exhibit 6.6, foundation philanthropy declines about one year after a major market decline. This is because foundations make giving commitments a year in advance of full cash distribution. Hence, a reduction in commitments that lead to a reduction in giving is not felt until an economic downturn has settled in. Indeed, in some cases, the economy turns up as foundation giving continues to fall, again because the lag between commitment and cash outflow does not respond rapidly to rapidly changing markets.

As noted in earlier chapters, the nonprofit sector is very much an economic engine. Little work is available that assesses the link between economic slowdowns and the strength of the sector in the economy. Some studies, although narrow, seem to indicate that nonprofits actually hold up better than commercial entities in difficult economic times. In the downturn of 2000–2003, surveys indicated that 80 percent of nonprofits did not experience workforce reductions.[8] Indeed, by 2003, the nonprofit sector in New York City had added 12,000 jobs, a 1.9 percent growth rate, while the private commercial sector had lost 8,700 jobs, or a 0.3 percent decline.[9]

Disaggregating to the Level of State Economies

Just as disaggregating data to the structure of giving and searching for matched economic measures is helpful in understanding the link between economic downturns and nonprofit strategies, so is it helpful to disaggregate geography. Although some extremely large nonprofits operate programs

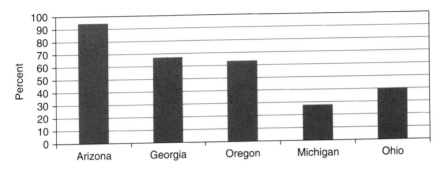

EXHIBIT 6.7 Change in Gross State Product, 1997–2007

Source: Bureau of Economic Analysis, Department of Commerce.

only at a national level, most nonprofits are tied to their communities or states. Their workers, their services, their donors are all bounded by geography. Most giving is local. Only 2 percent of giving flows to international causes. Most nonprofits are local. So it is reasonable to hypothesize that the health and directions of a state economy may be a better predictor of nonprofit economic health than the economic directions measured by national data. Again, rarely do commentators on the nonprofit sector make such disaggregated distinctions.

To examine the hypothesis, the author selected three states with robust economies over the past two decades, Arizona, Georgia, and Oregon, and two states that have faced prolonged economic challenges in that period, Michigan and Ohio. While the relationship between giving and GDP trends is mixed and even opaque, does the direction of economic indicators at the state level track more closely to giving behavior? Should nonprofit strategy that is sensitive to economic prospects first start at home, not at the level of national economic trends?

The difference in economic growth among the five states is striking, as illustrated in Exhibit 6.7. Arizona, Georgia, and Oregon have attracted and grown new industries, creating significant numbers of jobs over the last decade. Gross state product (GSP) rose by 60 percent or more. In Arizona, the state economy has nearly doubled in only the last 10 years. The recession of 2008–2009 represented a significant challenge for Arizona, but its decadal growth is nonetheless notable. In contrast, Michigan and Ohio have lagged, failing to attract new industries while old industries gradually withered.

A similar difference is seen when viewed not from the perspective of the economy but from the perspective of individual incomes. As noted previously, the individual household as a level of analysis is particularly apt for

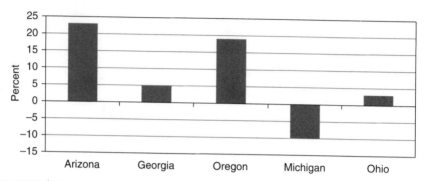

EXHIBIT 6.8 Change in Taxable Annual Wages, 2001–2007
Source: Bureau of Labor Statistics.

philanthropic assessments since more than four-fifths of giving originates with individuals. In the case of the five selected states, noted in Exhibit 6.8, taxable annual wages in Arizona and Oregon soared in the 2001–2007 period, while Michigan and Ohio lagged. Although the deep recession of 2008–2009 affected all states, the state budget deficits of Michigan and Ohio reached between $1.2 billion and $1.4 billion by March 2009. The state budget deficit in Oregon was $145 million. Unemployment in Michigan was 10.6 percent by that point, and in Ohio it was 7.8 percent. In Arizona, it was 6.9 percent. In Ohio, home foreclosures reached 4 percent; in Oregon, only 1.3 percent of homes were in foreclosure. Clearly, while the entire nation suffered from the 2008–2009 recession, in states like Ohio and Michigan, already weak economies buckled under the intense pressure of the downturn.

Are those very different state patterns repeated in the economic health of nonprofits and in personal philanthropy at the state level? There are several measurement dimensions for pursuing the inquiry. It is important to begin, however, by acknowledging the degree to which philanthropy and the nonprofit sector has grown in all five states in the last decade. Even in Michigan, arguably one of the states with the greatest economic stress, growth is seen in all nonprofit measures, from numbers of nonprofits to amount of revenue to the average contribution on an itemized tax return. What is striking in some ways is how similar the state level is to the national level. Philanthropy is amazingly resilient. Even in difficult economic times, which for Michigan and Ohio have lasted for many years, there is a continued commitment of citizens to use their discretionary income—even as that income itself declines—to support the common good. It is a testament to the nation's civil society that this is so clearly true.

That having been said, it is also clear that economic health at the state level is correlated with nonprofit strength. Let us take three measures: (1) the number of charities, (2) their revenue growth, and (3) individual giving.

Numbers of Charities

The number of charities in Arizona and Georgia has grown much more significantly than in the other states. Between 1995 and 2008, the number of nonprofits in Arizona doubled and in Georgia the increase was 147 percent. In Michigan, the number of charities increased by 87 percent, but in Ohio the number grew only by 68 percent in those 13 years.

What is more striking is the revenue trend. Here the analyst must be cautious. A huge public university such as Georgia Tech or Ohio State receives contributions from across the nation. Its revenues say little about the economic–nonprofit link between the people of Georgia or Ohio and their charities. To simply look at the contributions to in-state nonprofits without correcting for out-of-state contributions would be exceedingly misleading.

Patterns of Revenue Growth

Let us look for patterns in the revenue growth of public charities net of extremely large institutions with national fund-raising reach. There is no perfect way to carry out such an analysis, and no way to comprehensively and longitudinally sort through "revenue" to ensure that only in-state resources are being counted. If nonprofit revenue nets out extremely large institutions, the sample may better reflect the relationship between in-state giving and in-state nonprofits. The result of the effort is imperfect for many reasons, not the least of which is the inability to net out government grants from all grant dollars received. Nevertheless, even a flawed effort does suggest a pattern. As seen in Exhibit 6.9, in each of the three economically better-off states, nonprofit revenues of small and medium-sized nonprofits more than doubled; neither Michigan nor Ohio enjoyed such growth.

Individual Giving

A third view of the correlation can be taken from the perspective of private giving. Again, the data are not perfect. Indeed, it is extremely difficult to compare behavior by tax returns because there is such difference in the number of filers who itemize. If we limit our assessment only to those who itemize, and comment only on itemizers, however, we can avoid over-generalizing about state comparisons. Limited in this fashion, and as illustrated in Exhibit 6.10, in the decade 1995–2005, the growth in contributions per itemized tax return in Arizona, Georgia, and Oregon exceeded the

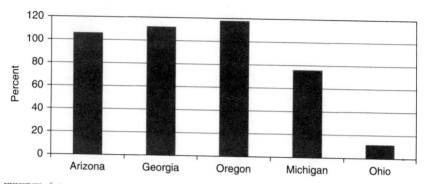

EXHIBIT 6.9 Revenue Increase in Nonprofits with Assets Less than $100 Million, 1995–2008

Source: NCCS.

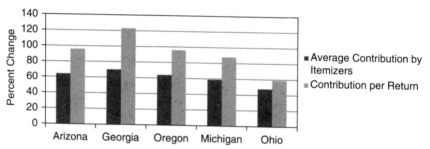

EXHIBIT 6.10 Change in Individual Giving by State, 1995–2005

Source: Center for Charitable Statistics.

growth in Michigan and Ohio. Indeed, in Ohio the average contribution of itemizers increased just 48 percent in current dollars, and considerably less in inflation adjusted dollars.

The general condition of the state economy correlated with the growth of contributions from those who itemized gifts on their tax returns.

Summary

The state perspective helps us understand the nonprofit–economy relationship. Analysis at the aggregate level of the nation may be washing out the relationships that actually do exist at the level of individuals and communities. While the results can only be tentative, given the small sample of states and the difficulties in gathering sufficiently longitudinal data, they do suggest that nonprofit revenue strategy, and especially the development of Early Warning Systems to trigger timely adjustment of strategy to accommodate economic turmoil, are most productive if they are sensitive to state-level data.

A Note on Government Roles

In testimony to the importance of revenue diversification to these trends, a study by the Nonprofit Finance Fund in 2008 found that over-dependence on government financing was associated with the greatest financial weakness in a recession. Nonprofits dependent on government money were more likely to face financial deficits and to recover more slowly than those that were not. In 1999, 39 percent of government-dependent nonprofits had deficits, a portion that rose to 55 percent in 2003 compared to 20 percent of all nonprofits surveyed. By 2005, the portion of largely government-funded nonprofits with deficits remained at 51 percent.[10]

It is important to recall the discussion in Chapter 3, "Philanthropy within Financial Structures," about the rise of government grants and contracts for program services within the structure of nonprofit revenue. Although such funding can provide diversification, when government funding itself begins to dominate revenue patterns, problems ensue, particularly in recessions when government budgets themselves are under stress. On the one hand, government payments themselves weaken. On the other hand, cost-reimbursement contracts for services do not allow nonprofits to build reserves. The government reimburses actual costs; unspent money must be returned. Consequently, overreliance on government spending launches a nonprofit into a financial vacuum during recessionary times.

Five Insights to Guide Strategic Directions

One of the great difficulties in understanding the relationship between economic change and philanthropy is the poor state of this type of analysis in the nonprofit sector. Few analyses disaggregate giving data. Fewer still reach deeper than macroeconomic measures.

Therefore, when a deep and long recession occurs, such as that experienced in 2008–2009, there are few places to turn for strategic guidance. The depth of the 2008–2009 recession has few precedents. A typical recession lasts nine months; the recession of 2008–2009 is projected to last 16 to 18 months. Unemployment spiked to near double digits and rose as high as 12 to 15 percent for a period in some communities. Consumer spending fell more rapidly than had been anticipated, and economists feared deflation, a period in which falling consumption leads to falling prices inhibiting any rise in profitable output. The credit system froze in the clutches of trillions of dollars of bad debt, impeding business and consumer lending and, indeed, the operational stability of nonprofits themselves.

Concern among nonprofits was deep and abiding. Nearly all nonprofits, from the smallest soup kitchen to the largest hospital, saw demand for

The Responsibility of an Investment Manager

Writing about joint stock companies in "The Wealth of Nations," Adam Smith notes that, as "managers . . . of other people's money . . . it cannot well be expected that they should watch over it with the same anxious vigilance with which the partners in a private (partnership) frequently watch over their own . . . Negligence . . . therefore, must always prevail . . ."

Though published in 1776, Smith's commentary undoubtedly applies to the 2008–2009 "crisis of ethic proportions" as exemplified by the post-Madoff world. This resonance underscores the critical need for a "fiduciary society" in which individuals, institutions, and nonprofit organizations are investors. As nonprofits rethink how they connect with donors, and as they develop new ways to generate income, those who manage the assets of nonprofits—foundations or endowments—must hold themselves to the highest standard of fiduciary duty.

What guidelines do investment managers need to implement in managing money for nonprofits, especially in times of economic downturn? Of fundamental importance is a soundly developed asset allocation that takes account of long-term strategic goals, as well as tactical operations that effect timely readjustments to the overall strategic plan. Investment managers must also be prepared to customize tactical changes to ensure that each client's portfolio accurately reflects the investor's risk tolerance. Finally, fiduciaries have a duty to perform thorough due diligence on all third-party managers and to provide straightforward reporting techniques that present results in a transparent manner.

Implementing an investment strategy that can preserve the purchasing power of an investment portfolio, accommodate annual spending needs, and assure sufficient liquidity is essential to weathering an economic downturn. Although each investor's solution represents a high degree of customization, a properly diversified investment approach that provides appropriate tactical responses can allow fiduciaries to meet the high standards of duty they owe to their clients.

Morgan Stanley Foundation and Endowment Services Coverage Team
James W. Burns, Managing Director
Cheryl MacLachlan, Executive Director
Stephanie A. Whittier, Executive Director
Christine L. Galib, Client Coverage
Lauren J. McDermott, Client Coverage

services and for financial help rise. In an already weakened economy, such as that of Michigan, nearly 80 percent of nonprofits saw service demand increase in October 2008 over a year before.[11] In such circumstances, there are no instant solutions to revenue crises. Without preexisting strategy that has prepared for economic cycles, there are few immediate options for bolstering balance sheets weakened both by state budget shortfalls and falling incomes. History teaches that there is no substitute for clear advance planning. The key learning from past relationships of philanthropy and nonprofit finance to the economy is fivefold.

First, for foundations, the challenge is to decide what business they are in. Severe and extended market downturns will, in fact, have a negative effect on foundation assets. The temptation is to extend that negative effect to grant making, in turn constricting nonprofit financial options. A longer-term view can preserve grant making and protect assets. Let us examine a hypothetical situation.

The Ajax Foundation has $10 million in assets and distributes 5 percent in grants as in accordance with the minimum required by the law. Market decline reduces its asset base by 16 percent to $8.4 million. Continued distribution at only the legal limit would reduce its grant making by $80,000. However, a one-year increase to 6 percent would return grant making to $504,000, costing only $84,000 to the asset base, an amount that could be restored by a 1 percent market gain.

For philanthropy, then, significantly stressed markets do, indeed, affect the capital base in the near term. A longer-term view, however, can result in near-term strategies that both help nonprofits weather economic downturns and protect the philanthropies in their long-term missions.

Second, corporate philanthropy does tend to plateau in times of economic challenge. As noted in Exhibit 6.11, in a survey in January 2009—in

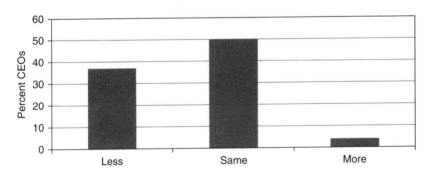

EXHIBIT 6.11 Corporate CEO Views on 2009 Direction of Corporate Giving
Source: LBG Research Institute.

a period with projections of at least 6 to 8 more months of economic decline—half of all executives interviewed intended to keep philanthropy at its historic levels and just over a third planned on reductions. With the stock market having lost 40 percent of its value and unemployment nearing 10 percent, it is striking that corporate intentions were so heavily to hold philanthropy steady. Those intentions often did not hold true to final corporate budgets, but they may bode well for a fairly rapid recovery in corporate philanthropic spending as recession eases.

But, as noted in earlier chapters, corporate "philanthropy" itself is evolving, and tightened economies may present more not fewer opportunities for nonprofits to craft corporate relationships. Consumer awareness of corporate social engagement and the previously cited propensity to bias spending toward brands that show social responsibility or that are aligned with societal needs is growing. As market competition tightens in a stressed economy, the need to compete may deepen rather than weaken nonprofit-corporate relationships, albeit through marketing not philanthropy budgets.

This is an important point and deserves emphasis. Corporate philanthropy, denominated in cash transfers from foundations or giving budgets, can only be as robust as the corporate bottom line itself. Philanthropy is a direct product of that bottom line. But this is an exceedingly narrow and an increasingly unjustified view of corporate social engagement. Many corporations take a "whole-of-corporation" approach to their social engagement. Demand for social programs and responsiveness actually grows in difficult economic cycles. Employees expect engagement. Competitive markets filled with educated consumers demand it. So even when the supply of philanthropic cash falls, rising demand leads the corporation to mobilize other types of resources to respond to demand—marketing budgets, employee engagement, executive time, and expertise. The nonprofit that takes a "cash only" view of corporate social engagement response to an ailing economy misses the complexity of the opportunity.

Third, revenue diversity is central to nonprofit stability. However, and this is a big however, the complexity of revenue diversification will not yield to panic. As will be noted in Chapter 7, "A Systems Approach to Revenue Strategy," a central lesson from past research on the link between economic downturns and nonprofits is that there is no substitute for revenue planning that takes place in advance of the crisis of the economic moment.

Fourth, specifics matter. What is true at the level of micro-analysis—the status of the state economy within which the nonprofit exists, the status of unemployment within the community to which the nonprofit turns for support—is infinitely more important to strategy development than the general state of the national or global economy. Strategy cannot be divined from nonstrategic macroeconomic data. Strategy must begin with, and regularly return to, the specifics of the economy within which the nonprofit operates.

Balancing Mission and Financial Strength

The strength of the United States is most admired and at its best when we properly balance our capitalist objectives with a strong sense of social responsibility. It is perhaps what Alexis de Tocqueville was commenting on in his major work *Democracy in America*, when he wrote about democracy as an equation that balanced liberty and equality. I believe this same balance exists in the most successful nonprofit organizations.

Leadership in the nonprofit world, to be successful, must balance the desire to improve society with the need to remain financially viable. As chairman of the international relief agency Concern Worldwide U.S. (www.concernusa.org), I understand that there is value in my leadership only so long as I also respect the value of the leadership provided by my executive director. The executive director, who is closely aligned with the community being served, must have a strong voice in representing the societal needs addressed in the mission and values of the organization. The chairman of the board and the directors at Concern Worldwide U.S. provide support to the executive director and management while challenging them to maintain the discipline needed to assure the financial strength and efficiency of the organization.

The board of directors and management must work in a collegial environment while still being encouraged to challenge each other. The passion of management and the benefit to the community must be shared so that the directors might develop their own passion for the mission and values. Working together to find the right balance between capitalism and social responsibility will provide rich rewards for the board of directors, management, staff, and, most important, the community being served. With this balance of interests comes commitment and dedication, which will ensure the survival of the organization no matter what the economic circumstances might be.

Thomas J. Moran
Chairman
Concern Worldwide U.S.
Chief Executive Officer
Mutual of America

Fifth, no sustained successful plan was ever developed in panic. The lesson for the nonprofit sector is clear. Economies are cyclical. They will decline. They will rise. The amplitudes of the cycles will differ, but they will happen. The time to develop financial strategies that adjust to cycles, that use declines as points of innovative opportunity not as points of despair, is not in the throes of recession. The time to develop such plans is now, and the time to reconsider and reassess those plans is regularly. Nonprofits must learn to predict their environment, not react to it. They must learn to act more like commercial entities—not in jettisoning their missions or their commitments but in anticipating hard times and planning for them. And those plans should be not simply to survive but rather to use decline as a mechanism for renewal, for identifying the old and worn and innovating with the new and forward-looking.

There is no market that will make nonprofits do this. There is no regulation that insists upon it. Wisdom is a quality, not a mandate. But history teaches that the wise nonprofit will expect change and, in expecting it, embrace it for the innovation and the renewal it can promise.

Notes

1. U.S. Small Business Administration. www.sba.gov/smallbusinessplanner/plan/getready/SERV_SBPLANNER_ISENTFORU.html.

2. Traditionally defined, a recession is a period of at least two consecutive quarters of a real (i.e., inflation adjusted) decline in the gross domestic product (GDP). The National Bureau of Economic Research has revised this definition to include more refined measures of the peak and valley of business activity. By that definition, the average recession lasts a year. Until the 1930s, any economic downturn was called a depression. Currently, the term "depression" usually refers to any economic downturn in which real GDP declines by 10 percent or more. By this definition, the two U.S. depressions were August 1929 to March 1933, when GDP declined by 33 percent, and May 1937 to June 1938, when GDP declined by 18.2 percent.

3. "Philanthropy in Uncertain Times: A Retrospective 1931–1949." Robert F. Sharpe and Company, 1992. This report is based on historical data from James Price Jones and F. Emerson Andrews.

4. Data files from the Internal Revenue Service. Previous years are available, but changes in the way in which household expenditures were defined and measured makes comparability difficult.

5. "The 2008 Study of High Net Worth Philanthropy." The Center on Philanthropy at Indiana University (March 2009), 39.

6. Indiana University, Op cit., 5–8.

7. S. Lawrence and R. Mukai. *Foundation Growth and Giving Estimates. Current Outlook 2009 Edition.* (Washington, DC: The Foundation Center, 2009).

8. G. Bernacchi, "Nonprofits Weathering Economic Story, Recession: NPT Survey Shows Steady Workforce." *The Non-Profit Times* 15:24 (December 15, 2001), 1.

9. T. Fredrickson, "Nonprofit Jobs Soaring: Recession Boosts Need." *Crain's New York Business* 19:49 (December 8, 2003) 1.

10. H. Hall, "Charities That Faced Deficits in Last Recession Are Still Trying to Recover." *Chronicle of Philanthropy* 20:9 (February 21, 2008), 1.

11. W. Miller, "Michigan's Nonprofits Struggle with Economic Downturn." Michigan Nonprofit Association and Johnson Center at Grand Valley State University, November 2008, 1.

CHAPTER 7

A Systems Approach
to Revenue Strategy

The essence of strategy is that you must set limits on what you are trying to accomplish.

Michael Porter

The previous chapters have depicted the degree to which revenue in the charitable sector has become complex and entangled with government as well as commercial and social markets. What is lacking is any organized manner by which to begin to develop strategy against complexity. A recipe for chaos and, ultimately, failure is to try to address all opportunities simultaneously. Strategy requires organizations to make choices, and choices require a way to organize complexity into decisionable patterns.

Thematic Summary

The complexity of changes in the definition of philanthropy and the complexity of nonprofit revenue structure call for careful attention to forward-looking strategies to strengthen revenue. However, complexity can impede strategy. Not every opportunity is correctly sized for every nonprofit. The number, size, and variety of trees easily distracts from plotting a path through the forest. In the nonprofit sector, the challenge is more complex because organizational eyes are normally turned inward to the constancy of mission, not outward to the edges of change. What is needed is an analytic framework that will enable strategies to be derived that scale from the most basic to the most sophisticated opportunities for creating long-term revenue that can survive the stress of deep economic turmoil.

How can what is ideally optimal be distinguished from what is practically possible? How can a nonprofit begin to organize its thinking about systems for revenue strengthening? Where to begin?

The Imperative of Letting Go: Paradigmatic Shifts

The place to begin is by letting go. This is understandably difficult. It generates nervous side glances and the frequent examination of the toes of one's shoes. Nevertheless, the creation of new analytic systems requires letting go of old analytic systems, old assumptions, and old, tattered blankets of comfort. There is no point in spending the time to conceive of new systems that correspond to new realities if it is the old ways that we clasp to our chests in fear.

Fear is not an uncommon response to the new, especially when the new is difficult to grasp and master. In 1962, Thomas Kuhn authored a short but dense and complex book entitled *The Structure of Scientific Revolutions*. It was a seminal work, and so elicited equal parts of admiration and fear.

Kuhn posited that progress in science takes place because fundamental paradigms shift. That is, over time, facts that are observed to be true do not match previous predictions about those facts. Gradually, a whole new worldview emerges that overturns previous approaches and practices and leads to new understanding. In Kuhn's view, this is not a matter of additions to traditional views, but rather the emergence and gradual acceptance of an entirely different conceptualization of how the world works.

What revenue strategy must accommodate is an analytic framework that is premised on a paradigmatic shift in philanthropy. The shift is not about money. It is about the entire structure of thinking and approach to problem solving.

To examine this thesis, let us begin with the definition of a paradigm. The word is so widely misused, largely because it is applied to relatively trivial change, in part, perhaps, so that observers and commentators seem smarter than the change warrants. In fact, a paradigm shift entails a very consequential change.

A paradigm comprises the underlying basis for a discipline or an area of inquiry. It is the acknowledged worldview of those who work in this area; it organizes and guides the definition of problems and the ways in which problems are approached. It defines what is expected and what is unexpected, and places the latter on the margins. Paradigms govern inquiry and beliefs. A paradigm is not a theory; it is the entire architecture that defines the subject matter for theory.

How do paradigms shift? Kuhn posits that change takes place when someone somewhere attributes value to anomalies. Why do I observe something happening that should not happen? What is the nature of this oddity

The Tsunami after the Perfect Storm

While most of the independent sector is "battening down the hatches" in hopes of riding out "the perfect storm" of economic crisis, a tsunami of seismic change is brewing just below the surface, which will have profound implications for the sector. Our boats may well weather the storm of the economic crisis, but if we want to also survive the tsunami of change we may want to consider abandoning our boats altogether—in favor of a surfboard.

We have some work to do if we want to survive. We must change the way we do business—including the way we define ourselves as non-profit organizations. This means diversification of revenue—including sources outside traditional fund-raising. It means creating a new type of business model that addresses quality management, competition, and outcomes as extensively as traditional business plans cover revenue generation and tracking.

Philanthropy wants results; so those of us on the front lines are under pressure to deliver. Adding to the pressure is the additional demand that we contribute *solutions* to the problems to which we currently only *respond*. All of these pressures are entirely justified. If we respond well, we will pass on to the next generations institutions of which they can be proud. However, we can only solve complex social problems if we first solve the problems unique to our sector.

Open Hand, Atlanta provides an illustration of that difficulty. We have been truly fortunate to have innovative, diverse funding sources, yet our progress has still been slowed by the problems endemic to our sector as a whole. Our social enterprise venture has contributed significant revenue to our mission and all but eliminated our quality management and cash flow constraints. We have been rewarded with a good reputation; yet we have difficulty demonstrating the "urgent need" for funding often required from traditional funding sources. We have created a business model structured for collaboration as opposed to competition; yet potential partners are slow to take advantage of it. We have created a cooperative bidding system and technology plan based on proven franchise models in the for-profit sector offering significant savings to our peers throughout the country; but we have no nonprofit association with whom to share it. We have created a system for capturing and tracking both financial and social impact that demonstrated the contribution to solutions. While verbally encouraged, the result is punishment by national organizations that rate charities on administration to program ratios. We have gone to great lengths to unravel the maze of red tape required to access stimulus funding because the

(Continued)

(*Continued*)

independent sector did not have a viable resource to consult. I point out these issues not to discourage innovation but to demonstrate the need for every member of the nonprofit sector to take responsibility for fixing what is not working and to celebrate what does work.

If it is true that significant change is only likely to happen when there is sufficient environmental momentum to propel it forward and a corresponding dissatisfaction with the status quo, I would say that time is now and the window is short.

Stephen Woods
Executive Director
Open Hand

and why does it not fit within the framework of my assumptions? Why does the paradigm not accept it? Why is this oddity clearly present on the map of my observations of the world, but the map, governed by the paradigm, does not recognize it as being there? How is it possible that people are not seeing what is so clearly true?

We cannot, of course, push Kuhn's analysis too hard. It was developed to understand scientific progress. Philanthropy is not science. But there is an analogous case to be made for the variations of resource flows on the societal commons that we have long called "charity" or "philanthropy" or "donations" to "nonprofits."

Historically and largely still, philanthropy is about the transfer of money from the individual with it to the individuals without it. The currency behind the relationship is that of a gift or a voluntary transfer of value from giver to recipient without compensation. The gift is premised on resource redistribution to help those in need. The framework is the intersection of the individual with resources and his or her particular interests and the solicitation of a particular organization in that area of interest who needs (or wants) those resources. The individual philanthropist and the individual nonprofit are the units of analysis. The objective is support of the work of the nonprofit. The overall culture is one of gifting by donors to recipients; donors give money, recipients receive money. Demanding donors may require information in return for their money, but information is not embedded in the gifting relationship.

In essence, the relationship and the culture are asymmetrical. The relationship is not one of mutuality of responsibility and accountability, but one of giver and receiver. The explanation for the relationship is the power of generosity hotwired into the American spirit; givers will give because they see need, and they will give as required to resolve need.

Since 1966, $5.5 trillion has changed hands on this basis. The number of public charities has increased by 200 percent in the last two decades; the inflation adjusted dollar value of philanthropy has increased by 150 percent.

But the anomalies in the paradigm are becoming clearer. With $5.5 trillion dollars flowing to 8.5 percent of the U.S. economy, there are objects on the map that the paradigm cannot explain. Despite the flow, for example, most nonprofits remain small and financially weak, regularly endangered by a turn of philanthropic fortunes. Despite the growth in resources, fundamental social problems continue apace, showing little progress for the dollars spent. The portion of GDP or household income allocated to philanthropy has not risen much above 2.2 percent nor fallen much below 1.7 percent since records have been kept. Nonprofits are not growing apace with problems, and philanthropy is not growing beyond a fixed portion of economic capacity. The anomaly is that we have growth without the progress that growth is supposed to create. In classic paradigm-shifting terms, we have an outcome other than that which we would expect.

New observers are seeing this anomaly and are shifting the paradigm. As in all paradigm shifts, a new view is not easily or readily accepted by the existing view, either because it is poorly understood or because it threatens existing interests or capacities. Remember, a paradigm is not a theory or a set of tasks; it is the entire worldview that a discipline or sector brings to its understanding of the worth of its work and it defines the fundamental nature of problems to be addressed. It is not surprising, then, that a change in paradigm is rarely smooth and never welcomed with open arms.

But it is this shift that an analytic framework must accommodate, because it is this shift that gives rise to the diversity of opportunity for revenue strengthening that nonprofit strategy must accommodate and exploit.

We cannot have robust strategy if we do not have an accurate and comprehensive framework of analysis. And we cannot have an accurate and comprehensive framework if we do not understand the paradigm shift undergirding the new reality. In discussing the new methods to flow funds to the societal commons in previous chapters, we have presented some of the new approaches that reflect a change in perspective of what the nonprofit sector is, how it should operate, and how it relates to the rest of the human and financial resource base of a society.

The Shifting Basis for Strategy

In sum, there are five dimensions of this shift that affect the framework through which revenue must be seen, and hence the strategies by which revenue can be strengthened.

First, the loyalty in the new paradigm is not between the giver and the receiver (let us use these terms for now; they are amended below); the loyalty is to the problem. The philanthropist focuses not on the nonprofit receiving resources, but on the problem being solved. If nonprofit A cannot demonstrate that it can solve the problem, nonprofit B is just as likely to be supported. The question then is not "Do you do good work?" but "Can you demonstrate that you can fix the problem?" Donor and receiver do not sit across from each other; they sit together and together are focused on problem solving.

Second, therefore, the new paradigm seeks solutions. The problem on the societal commons is not a lack of money so much as it is a lack of demonstrable solutions to problems. The new money does not seek to transfer resources to help; it seeks to transfer resources to "fix it."

Third, the new paradigm does not think of resource transfer as a matter of gifts. The new paradigm uses an investment model, either in fact or by analogy. In its most innovative forms, the new paradigm seeks to flow resources to problems in ways that create sustained institutional capability and force accountability to the funder. Even gifts come with the language of investment, expecting quantifiable social and economic returns. The assumption is that an investment culture will result in more disciplined allocation of resources to problem solving than a gifting culture.

Fourth, the new paradigm seeks scale because most problems cannot be demonstrably resolved except at scale. Consequently, the new paradigm values collaboration. Philanthropists in the new paradigm do not see the world through a straw—a singular relationship between philanthropist and nonprofit. Rather, they seek to combine individual philanthropic resources toward a mutually perceived problem and use their collaboration to incentivize collaboration among nonprofits and across problem areas. With scale defined as a problem, the investment culture seeks partner collaboration in both funding and execution.

Fifth, because partnership is essential to scale, the new paradigm values mutuality of problem definition and program execution. "Engaged philanthropy" is a widely used and poorly understood phrase. To nonprofits, it often implies meddling; to philanthropists, it can mean control. More often, it means exactly what it says, a convenient characteristic of most words. The new paradigm places peer relationships at its cultural core. Philanthropists are not checkbooks; nonprofits are not forever dependent. Planning flows both ways, information flows both ways, strategy for sustainability flows both ways. Nonprofits retain and maximize their technical knowledge and educate philanthropists; philanthropists use their organizational, managerial, financial, and other expertise to help develop actionable strategies. Accountability is mutual; transparency is valued.

What happens when two paradigms clash? Kuhn's thesis is that, in science, both cannot coexist. The emerging paradigm redefines the nature of inquiry and the nature of reality such that it replaces old ways, old questions, and old modes of thinking. We cannot have a world in which it is equally true that the sun revolves around the earth and the earth revolves around the sun. One must replace the other; both cannot be accurate depictions of reality.

Here, the Kuhn model breaks down, but that should give us little comfort.

It is true that pure asymmetrical giving will continue to exist, at least in part because it is appropriate to the nature of some of the problems that the societal commons faces. For many problems—disasters, for example—the mere fact that we as a species share a common genome and a common right to human dignity calls out for generosity for its own merit. There are myriad reasons for giving for giving's sake. That a new paradigm is emerging for complex problems with deep roots and global import based on the growing perception of the need for sustained and sustainable investment does not obviate those reasons.

However, the emergence of that new paradigm does require that space be made for it in the world of nonprofit finance. The new paradigm implies new skills, new relationships, new pathways of accountability, new standards of performance, and new criteria for decision making. These imply a very, very different kind of culture than in traditional gift-making approaches.

As with any paradigm shift, there is nervousness and even resistance to this new way of looking at the world. There is, in fact, good cause for such nervousness in the nonprofit world. In fact, there will be displacement. In many areas of endeavor, resources will not flow without conditions; philanthropists will no longer simply write checks; information will be expected and even demanded; strategies for philanthropic sustainability will be required. This will happen not just for new initiatives or new problems. It will happen for problems and with organizations that have long been part of the traditional paradigm. In tandem, new skills will be necessary, and they will bring new people and new educational methods to the sector. Gradually, these new skills will be expected of a greater and greater number of people in this sector.

The Context of an Analytic Framework for Strategy

The previous chapters have emphasized the evolving complexity of revenue in the nonprofit sector. That evolution has taken nonprofits from the early

The Transition of Nonprofits to Microfinance

Facilitating small loans to micro-entrepreneurs around the world, even where poverty is dominant, is not a new concept. Now, traditional non-profit organizations are turning to microfinance as a vehicle to leverage donor funds for a double bottom-line impact—as immediate financial resources to fund operations and as invested resources to build endowments for local capacity. Many nonprofit organizations with a purely charitable mission are confronting decreased contributions due to the current financial upheaval by turning to some for-profit concepts. However, this hybridization faces hurdles. Indeed, there are few organizations (Tier 1 category microfinance institutions [MFIs]) that have been able to play effectively in the nonprofit/for-profit space. The Achilles' heel is organizational maturity.

Achieving microfinance maturity reflects factors common to the traditional banking world. First, management maturity and discipline must increase. Nonprofits of all types are continually being evaluated on their management teams and board interactions. Treating the MFI like a business with appropriate metrics and financial transparency is paramount. Although it is often counter to nonprofit practice, the ability to openly discuss mission drift or financial upheaval is critical.

Second, the business model of a microfinance institution is based on large numbers of transactions. Operational metrics are critical. This demands a process focus by the MFI management to consider continuous improvement, process redesign, and best practices development.

Third, adopting a service-oriented mentality becomes more important. Satisfying a mission and providing goods for free often creates low expectations of service behavior. However, when distribution of funds is the mode of operation, nonprofits begin putting a price tag on the service (e.g., interest rates or "on-time" payments). This changes the relationship between organization and beneficiary, and new expectations and behaviors emerge. MFIs with a customer-service focus—more than a donations focus—experience lower loss ratios.

In times of economic uncertainty, nonprofits with broad reach can challenge existing financial institutions. When microfinance is banking "as it used to be," it becomes a resilient foundation for financial trust and value creation. The future is still bright for microfinance and the promise abounds.

Patricia Tyre
President
Pacific Global Investments, LLC

simplistic days of merely accepting private donations to fund their work to business entities (in the case of larger or more entrepreneurial organizations) with myriad sources of income. Exhibit 7.1 depicts the potential revenue complexity of a nonprofit with a full suite of revenue streams.

Traditional flows encompass grants and donations from individuals, including bequests, foundations, and corporations, as well as income flows from government grants and contracts and service fees. The latter represent some combination of fees from users and user costs subsidized through or reimbursed by government payments.

Innovations, discussed in previous chapters and noted in Exhibit 7.1 by the shaded boxes, have affected these flows in two ways. First, there can be increased conditionality attached to the transfers of resources. For example, increased expectations for measurement of impact may attach to a donor grant. This does not, however, change the basic nature of the transfer. Second, the definition of funder interests may change. For example, corporations now align their grant making more closely with their business

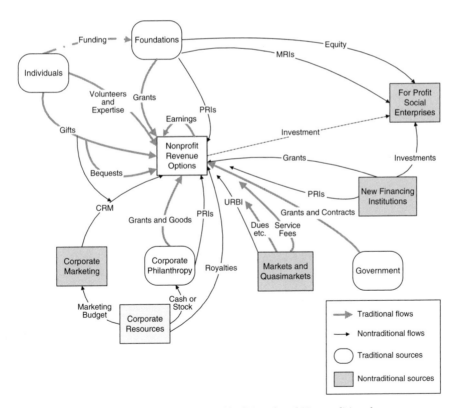

EXHIBIT 7.1 Flow of Nonprofit Revenue, Traditional and Nontraditional

interests and capacities. Again, this may introduce a different mix of sectors or topics of interest to the corporate grant maker, but it does not necessarily change the fundamental way in which resources are transferred.

More innovative flows, however, represent resources with structure or conditions that are fundamentally different from those of traditional donor resource transfers. Program-related investments, for example, apply to opportunities that have resource flows or other forms of collateral that will allow repayment. Cause-related marketing requires that nonprofit mission be directly related to corporate market opportunity.

These new flows, therefore, require at least three conditions.

First, nonprofits must be open to complying with the conditions placed on the transfers. Program-related investments, for example, mean a willingness to incur risk in exchange for relatively patient capital. Managers and boards of trustees need to be able to understand and accept that risk.

Second, management must have the capacity to manage the specific nature of the flows. Most nonprofit managers may not have commercial market skills that enable increases in market-driven goods or services. The skill base of the nonprofit can be a significant limiting condition on its ability to capitalize on the opportunity that comes with innovation. Strategy to seize innovation must include solutions for the skills that innovation demands

Third, for many of the opportunities, a nonprofit's culture must be entrepreneurial. The successful nonprofits of the future must breed entrepreneurship. Nearly all innovation requires constant change and adaptation. Today's strategy or idea is only as good as tomorrow's better idea. Change is difficult for all individuals. It induces an allergic reaction in most institutions. In the nonprofit sector, organizational eyes are normally turned inward to the constancy of mission—what we have earlier described as "mission as anchor"—not outward to the edges of change, which is "mission as sail." To see mission as sail is, effectively, to be comfortable in an entrepreneurial culture. Tom Harrison, in his seminar work on "entrepreneurial DNA," points out that entrepreneurs are "instinctive risk takers." It is, he says, "the love of what's next."[1] It is this kind of atmosphere that will characterize the successful nonprofit both in times of economic growth and economic retrenchment. Innovation in the face of opportunity requires being comfortable with seizing what's next.

It is clear that diversity creates complexity and complexity creates opportunity. The emergence of alternative concepts of revenue provides the robust nonprofit with many different options for crafting diverse revenue streams that, in turn, can provide stability through times of economic turbulence.

Therein lies the problem. It is equally clear that it is extremely difficult to think about strategy when the possible permutations and combinations of action are so great. Exhibit 7.1 may reflect the dimensions of opportunity. It does not constitute an analytic framework that will allow organizations

Planned Giving: The Nonprofit's Salvation in an Economic Downturn?

Planned giving is often touted as a "cure-all" for fund-raising challenges regardless of economic conditions. It is time to acknowledge a new reality: Investment losses such as those witnessed in late 2008 and early 2009 can be *catastrophic* to life-income programs.

Why? The most popular life-income vehicles promoted and managed by nonprofits are charitable gift annuities (CGAs) and charitable remainder annuity trusts (CRATs). Both guarantee fixed annual payments to income beneficiaries *regardless* of the status of the principal invested. If investments lose 30 percent or more in value in one year, the result is undeniable: *CGAs and CRATs will run out of money.* It may be 5 to 10 years away, but it is coming.

Reaching for greater investment returns is not the answer when doing so will only create greater risk!

Bringing in new gifts (CGAs in particular) to provide more cash flow is tantamount to running a charitable Ponzi scheme. Paying old obligations with money from new obligations is a losing proposition. It will drain the principal from the new obligations, which will in turn require organizations to go out and secure more new obligations, etc., etc., etc. Eventually, the whole fund will collapse.

So, is it time to bury our heads in the sand and hope that donors don't live out their life expectancies?

No, it is time to take an honest look at program obligations, recognize which gifts are in danger of exhaustion, and start talking to donors! And it is time to revisit our planned giving offerings, educate ourselves as to the risks involved, and adjust our gift acceptance policies.

Finally, it is time to fully appreciate the beauty of a simple bequest—still the most common, the most profitable, and arguably the most secure form of planned gift.

Mary Beth Martin, JD
Jonathan Gudema, JD
Changing Our World, Inc.

to begin to purposefully consider strategies for revenue enhancement and understand the organizational characteristics upon which each strategy is dependent. However accurate about the range of potential flows of resources, it does not help an organization stand in its current shoes and walk a manageable path forward to diversification. Indeed, it does not even help an organization decide whether moving forward is within its capacities or desires.

Proposed Analytic Framework to Organize Strategy

What is needed is an analytic framework. Let us begin with a clear understanding of what that is and why it is important.

An analytic framework is a tool to give discipline to discussion. It is a method for organizing data or observations so that their characteristics or dimensions can be understood in a systematic fashion. In this case, the purpose of the framework is not just to understand the dimensions of revenue options but to support an equally disciplined approach to developing and sorting strategies for action. Analytic frameworks are critical tools because they allow multiple factors and variables to be coherently organized so that their relationships can be understood. In the old adage of not seeing the forest for the trees, an analytic framework, in effect, allows us to assess each and every tree, and the relationships among the trees, while always armed with a complete view of the forest.

Exhibit 7.2 provides a proposed analytic framework to guide the development of revenue strategy aimed at strengthening nonprofits in anticipation of economic challenges. The framework accommodates changes in the definition of "philanthropy" as differing types of revenue flow onto the societal commons, and changes in the definition of "nonprofit" as more organizations combine elements of traditional giving with elements of commercial and financial markets and instruments.

This framework will provide the structure for the discussion of strategy in Chapters 8 through 10. Let us begin by reviewing its basic dimensions.

The analytic framework is constructed with two sets of intersection vectors that allow the characterization of organizations or types of finance and two sets of boundaries that set the conditions for strategy.

The Organizational or Finance Vectors

The framework arrays revenue options along two intersecting vectors. The horizontal vector represents a spectrum of organizational structure from pure nonprofit to pure for-profit. The vertical vector represents a spectrum of financing from pure donations to pure investment. The framework allows us to see the relative position of both organizational type and of financing type. Organizations increasingly have blends of charitable and commercial characteristics, and financing parameters and conditions also represent blends of dimensions or expectations about performance.

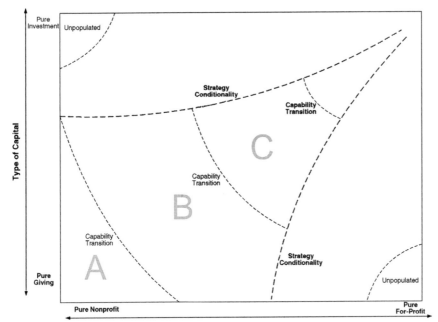

Type of Capital

Type of Organizational Structure

EXHIBIT 7.2 Basic Analytic Framework

A soup kitchen, dependent wholly on general cash donations, volunteer help, and donated food to serve the poor, would be found in the lower bottom left of the framework. It is a (relatively) purely charitable nonprofit relying purely on traditional philanthropic giving. A wind-power company, on the other hand, rests at the top-right corner of the framework. It is a purely for-profit commercial enterprise relying purely on investment and the markets for its resources, yet it operates on, or for the benefit of, the social commons. Combinations of types of nonprofits and hybrids of nonprofit and for-profit organizational models can be placed in the quadrants according to their mix of type and finance.

Similarly, types of financing can be placed in the quadrants. Again, anchoring the two ends of the spectrum helps to understand the different combinations that are possible. Traditional donations from individuals and (to some extent) foundations can be placed in the lower left of the framework. These are pure gifts to pure nonprofits. But giving also has emerging complexity. Pure gifts with no conditions are to be found in the lowest left of the framework. Giving (individual or foundation) that requires more business-like behavior or measurement moves more to the center of that framework because these gifts come with "strings" of conditions or expectations that require specific nonprofit behaviors in return.

On the other hand, the flow of royalties to nonprofits can be placed at the top right of the framework. These are funds that come to nonprofits from some type of license (or product or brand) that is only viable because of a commercial market. They are the product of pure market forces that are common to a purely for-profit organizational type. Again, combinations and hybrids of funding sources and strategies can be placed throughout the framework to reflect a mix of financing characteristics and purposes.

Using the framework in this way, one can plot the combinations that underpin various revenue diversification options and begin to think about their viability of appropriateness for the specifics of nonprofit mission and organization.

The Strategy Boundaries

But strategy does not derive from organizational type or the availability of revenue alternatives. Strategy must be developed by judgments within two sets of boundaries.

STRATEGY CONDITIONALITY   Various revenue options have boundary conditions, what I would call "strategy conditionality." Because an option is theoretically possible does not make it is tactically practical. As noted above, most innovations come with assumptions about financial structure, organizational mission, skill base, and risk propensities. As one moves from the lower left to the upper right of the framework, the degrees of freedom for strategy development narrow. The funding may become more robust, but the constriction on how it can be accessed and under what conditions (its "conditionality") grows. Hence, strategy for accessing and folding new revenue sources into the nonprofit's diversification portfolio plays on a narrower and narrower field. As well, the number and types of nonprofits that may be viable within that strategy also narrow.

Conditionality is critical to strategy for two reasons. First, the expectations of and parameters on some types of resources may not fit the revenue or mission structure of all nonprofits. Second, not all nonprofits will be comfortable conforming to the organizational dictates of all types of resources. The narrower area dictated by the conditionality border, the more careful a nonprofit must be in including that revenue option in its organizational strategy.

There is no firm and fast place along the strategy conditionality border for any particular financing option or for any particular organization. New dimensions of an existing strategy (e.g., program-related investment options that ease repayment expectations) can move a strategy into areas of the framework with less conditionality and greater maneuverability. Increased expectations about business practices associated with grant performance can move foundation grant making into more constrained areas of the framework.

Although the strategy conditionality band and its application are elastic, it is everywhere present. This is part of what makes strategy challenging in the nonprofit sector. Within the confines of the law, no-holds-barred may provide limitless strategy in the commercial sector. In the nonprofit sector, however, there is rarely a no-holds-barred option. All nonprofits hold some mission limitations and operate within some organizational culture and set of societal values. If they do not, their nonprofit status would be irrational. If all things are possible and all options are open in the marketplace, then there is no reason to operate an organization as a nonprofit and forego the benefits of distributing positive earnings to owners.

INTERNAL CAPACITY TRANSITION   Within the playing field created by the conditionality boundaries are transition points at which an organization must evolve from its skills, view of its mission, and expectations about its relationships with its revenue sources. These transition boundaries represent conscious decisions on the part of a nonprofit to develop or bring in the types of capacities that allow it to develop strategy for, and operate within, the playing field established by conditionality.

Exhibit 7.2 portrays these four dimensions—(1) type of capital, (2) type of structure, (3) conditionality, and (4) capacity transition—into a single system.

Strategic Area A, "Expressive Philanthropy," represents a playing field with wide leeway for the expansion of traditional "expressive" philanthropy. The term is widely used in the sector to refer to giving to nonprofits, which, as will be further discussed in Chapter 9 ("Getting Down to Specifics"), flows because of a shared sense of purpose and values between giver and recipient. This is funding that is a true gift, imposing no expectations on the recipient (even if the gift is tied to a particular purpose, such as a building or a program) beyond the use of the gift to advance the purpose of the nonprofit.

Strategy Area B, "Rising Expectations," represents funding sources that come with increasing concerns over alignment with their own internal priorities and increasing concern over documenting impact relative to those priorities. The highlight is not simply on shared concerns but on the specific nature of the funder's expectations and the need to demonstrate that those expectations are being met. The financial playing field begins to narrow and those that succeed begin to require different types of skills, especially impact and evaluation skills, and greater willingness to align not simply with shared values but with the specific priorities of funders.

Diversifying revenue into Strategy Area C, "Quasi Markets," begins to narrow the strategic options because funding comes with more and more conditionality and requires that organizations cross a transition barrier that requires different kinds of skills (e.g., more financial management capacity), different types of expectations (e.g., the repayment of program-related investments or alignment with corporate markets), and different types of relationships with funding sources (e.g., greater hands-on engagement of donors). Many of the revenue options in Strategy Area C mimic financing options in the commercial sector, which further drives the need for organizational capacity transition. Hence, diversification strategies come with a price in terms of the conditions attached to the funding and in terms of the internal capacity of the organization.

Diversifying further into Strategy Area D, "Markets," requires additional skills and additional limits. Financing strategies in Area D are exceedingly market sensitive and bring the nonprofit into a playing field that is exceedingly commercial in nature.

An organization that wishes to have a fully diversified approach to revenue must be able to live in all three areas at once, and develop and execute a wide variety of strategies.

Populating the Framework

Exhibit 7.3 populates this framework with examples of financing options discussed in prior sections of the book.

- *Strategy Area A* is populated with revenue flows that are purely traditional and purely gifts with few if any return expectations.
- *Strategy Area B* includes flows toward more conditional (but still grant-based) options like gifts premised on impact measures and corporate giving premised on corporate market profiles. Venture philanthropy, with clear expectations for outcomes and the philanthropist involved, begins to be introduced in this area. The playing area is large but begins to narrow as the capabilities boundary is approached.
- *Strategy Area C* contains revenue options with narrower conditionality and closer analogies to commercial finance requiring additional skill sets. Corporate social responsibility strategies, which require tighter coherence with corporate goals, venture philanthropy, which requires management of deeper philanthropist engagement, social enterprise, which requires business-like planning and management models, program-related investment, which requires both the capacity and the skill to treat philanthropy engagement as a loan not a grant and the skill to assess repayment risks.

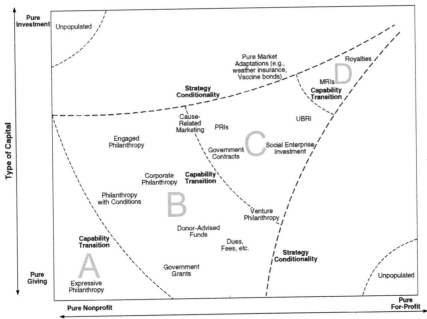

EXHIBIT 7.3 Revenue Populated Analytic Framework

- *Strategy Area D.* Approaching the second capabilities barrier, strategy options move to Area D. In Area D, conditionality is strong. Organizations must be able to behave similarly to commercial organizations, and must be willing and able to treat revenues as market driven. While potentially robust financially, these options require sophisticated strategy and equally sophisticated programs and organizations.

Clearly, developing diverse revenue streams is not simply a matter of gathering in money from "a bunch" of sources. The challenge for nonprofits is to develop strategies and associated skills and tactics that are both true to a nonprofit organization's societal mission and robust relative to the changing world of philanthropic definitions. The remaining chapters of this book will suggest such strategies within the framework of analysis that combines nonprofits, traditional giving, and marketlike resources.

Note

1. T. L. Harrison, *Instinct: Tapping Your Entrepreneurial DNA to Achieve Your Business Goals* (New York: Warner Business Books, 2005), 71–72.

CHAPTER 8

Common Principles
for Robust Strategy

Our work together to help the world's poor is more important in the face of this global financial crisis. If we lose sight of our long-term priority to expand opportunity for the world's poor and abandon our commitments and partnerships to reduce inequity, we run the risk of emerging from the current economic downturn in a world of even greater disparities . . .

Bill Gates, World Economic Forum,

Davos, 2009

In all economies, good, bad, and awful, everyone looks for leadership, for individuals who can forge a path forward. The key to leadership is motivating and inspiring people through passion based on valuing people, constant innovation, hard work, and excellence. There are general principles to be derived from these common elements of leadership.

Thematic Summary

The variety of nonprofits and the growing complexity of revenue sources mitigate against single or even simple strategies for nonprofit revenue strength in the face of economic turmoil. Complexity needs to beget complexity for opportunity to be maximized. Nevertheless, there are a series of fundamental strategic cores that anchor all revenue strategy in the nonprofit sector because they reflect the fundamental purpose
(Continued)

(Continued)

that all nonprofits share—engagement of citizens on the societal commons. From a common purpose can be derived a central strategic goal of engagement for which a series of four core strategic principles can be derived.

Previous chapters have emphasized the opportunity that is inherent in the emerging complexity of financial flows to the nonprofit sector. They have also emphasized that such complexity cannot be met with simplicity. No healthy economy grows constantly. No nonprofit faces a guaranteed future of adequate resources. Complex strategy is essential for nonprofits that wish to continually prepare themselves to face changing economic cycles and the evolving philanthropic marketplace.

One size does not fit all, however. Differences abound in the sector. There is no single set of actions that will provide stability and security to all nonprofits. We have seen that the umbrella term "nonprofit" now shelters a vast range of institutions of extraordinary diversity in size and mission. For each of these institutions, moreover, the "comfort level" of strategic conditionality will differ. Some will be more comfortable with the narrow expectations and high demands of innovative funding; some will not. This diversity works against generalization about strategic action.

Yet all nonprofits share (or ought to share) a common central purpose, the voluntary engagement of citizens in problem solving on the societal commons, the common effort to respond to needs that no one individual has sufficient motivation or capacity to address alone. There is a core to all revenue strategy, therefore, and that core is engagement. This is the prerequisite for the long-term viability of all other types of strategy—the engagement of individuals in the problem solving pursued by the nonprofit. Revenue strategies are important only insofar as they serve that role.

A Note on Mission

This point deserves additional comment. One can conceive of myriad ways to increase program revenues. For example, a better quality of napkin sold at the museum bookstore may yield higher prices and higher margins. In turn, higher margins may mean more money for the museum. There is certainly nothing wrong with such an effort—indeed, the combination of quality and clever marketing may be a real part of a multifaceted revenue strategy. There is clear merit to be had. But napkins alone do not a nonprofit make. For the nonprofit, the point of napkin sales is not to corner the napkin market.

Napkins are a means not an end. The point is not to sell napkins; the point is to support a mission on the societal commons, not a mission on the napkin market.

Underscoring the importance of mission is critical before proceeding so that the general strategic principles outlined below are not misunderstood. The mission of a nonprofit on the societal commons does not necessarily change with revenue strategy. What changes, however, may be its alignment with the operating environment and its execution through the embodiment of programs. That the mission is central to a nonprofit does not mean that it need be calcified. The strategic principles in this chapter assume the centrality of mission. However, they also assume that organizational embodiment of mission accommodates economic, demographic, and societal changes, indeed takes advantage of those changes. The mission of a college is education. Revenue strategy does not demand that the mission be changed to cement making. However, strategy may require that mission be pursued in different ways or with a different programmatic emphasis, as several examples below will note. This does not subsume mission to strategy, it aligns mission with the changes and opportunities on which strategy seeks to capitalize. Balance is required—between mission and change, between the past and the future, between tradition and innovation. But balance is not the same as immobility.

Acknowledging the centrality of mission, then, a series of common strategic principles, applicable to nonprofit strategy irrespective of the details of mission, can be posited.

Strategic Principle One: Value the People

The vast, vast majority of institutions come to believe deeply in themselves. Over time they become convinced that they, and they alone, hold the key to problem solving. Especially where there is competition for resources, the emphasis is on underscoring the uniqueness of internal expertise. The temptation to do so is even more intense in times of economic pressure. As resources constrict, that tendency intensifies. Let us be clear. Competition is a good thing; indeed it is the single greatest force that can propel institutions to higher levels of innovation. However, that force must be seized and embraced. If the organizational response is to emphasize internal expertise not external opportunity, to differentiate on the basis of what is inside an organization not how it relates to what is outside the organization, then an organization tends to focus on what it wants to do, what it sees as the priority.

All institutions, then, become inward looking over time. Most organizations become even more inward looking when they are under stress. This is not a characteristic of nonprofits alone. It is true of corporations. It is also true of governments. There is a natural instinct to pull in, to circle the wagons. For the nonprofit, however, it is a fundamental strategic error because the purpose of a nonprofit is not the assurance of its own existence. People do not voluntarily turn over their hard-earned, discretionary dollars to nonprofits so that nonprofits can continue to make payroll, however important payroll is. People support nonprofits because they expect nonprofits to solve the problems of people.

The first, foremost, and fundamental strategic principle, therefore, is to value the people. Nonprofits exist at the will of the people who are willing to shoulder the extra taxes (in some communities, as much as 50 percent of property is off the tax rolls because it is owned by nonprofits) in exchange for dedication to societal needs. The will of the people matters, and the people must be valued.

What are the embedded tactics inherent in this priority? First *listen*. Ask those who are served what they think of the services being provided. Understanding what the clients (students, poor families, the homeless, worshippers, donors, whomever) actually think, listening to those views, and reaching out ever more rigorously to meet those expectations is not only the antidote to dissatisfaction that spills over into the public arena, it is the only way to fulfill the core mission of engagement.

Ask those who donate what they think of the work, of the quality of communication, of the mission, of the effort to reach out and engage them in the work. Mayor Ed Koch of New York City was famous for using the opportunity of a broadcast interview to look into the camera and say to the voters, "How'm I doin'?" and so constantly take the temperature of supporters. Mayor Rudy Giuliani was an advocate of the 8 A.M. Monday morning meeting, a mechanism for constantly measuring and anticipating the external environment and aligning his city government to what had changed in the previous week and what needed to change to accommodate that change. For Mayor Giuliani, leadership required constant adaptation to change, and constant information and communication were critical to that adaptation.

The core lesson is relevant; ask your supporters what they think, and listen to what they say. This does not mean running willy-nilly hither and yon chasing each and every idea or option. It means listening and seriously sorting through those observations, always seeking insights, and using those insights to strengthen, and, yes, where appropriate, adjust mission, organization, and programs. Only asking will unveil the value proposition of the insights of supporters.

Beyond those you serve and those who support you, ask the community what they think of the work. Do they even know who you are? Do they even know what you do? Are there ways to deepen the engagement of

Assigning Value to Vision: The Critical Role of Communications in a Down Economy

No matter the economy, a good cause is hard to overlook. The challenge in today's marketplace is that donors are seemingly overwhelmed by good causes. I'd argue the single greatest investment a nonprofit organization can make today is on crafting and communicating clear, compelling, and differentiated messages that make it easy for donors to understand who you are, what you stand for, and how your offering is unique.

Easier said than done.

Because the nonprofit community spends its time and money implementing programs to make a difference, they often forget that they need to communicate why they exist in the first place. What problem had not been identified? What approach had not been explored? Where did you seek to succeed where others failed and why should a donor care?

Because these questions frequently go unanswered, organizations are—rightly or wrongly—lumped together as "disease fighters," "education groups," or "child savers." It may sound cynical, but in a down economy where donors are overwhelmed with "asks," it's easier for them to categorize and dismiss than to invest in uncovering the true value an organization provides, let alone relate to it.

The good news is that there is tremendous opportunity for nonprofits that embrace that reality and push themselves to articulate value in a way that sets them apart from the pack. The steps are simple, but the process is challenging, as those involved must be intensely critical of themselves and simultaneously respectful of others.

For organizations ready to invest in finding their niche and articulating their value in focused, relevant, and donor-friendly ways the reward is clear—greater clarity of mission and vision that serves internal and external audiences alike. Challenging yourself to differentiate your message and articulate your unique value means the end of being categorized and dismissed and the beginning of true donor engagement.

Leslie Tullio
Brodeur Partners

the average citizen? As has been noted, the community pays the taxes of the nonprofits that serve the societal commons. The community's view is central to the credibility of the nonprofit. Listen to what the community says and constantly improve.

The result will be a greater propensity of the community, its leaders, and its citizens to consider the value of a nonprofit's work and, therefore, ultimately provide the human and financial resources necessary for its mission.

For corporations, such constant market assessment is a matter of course. Without constant realignment to changing views, commercial products and services wither. If the market view has changed, then the corporation naturally either adjusts the product or seeks to adjust the view. Nonprofits seem to think such assessments are less important. This is perhaps because nonprofits focus on the merits of their mission, on the good that they do, and assume that those missions supersede what people think. And that, if by chance a negative view exists, it is the people who are wrong. Effective revenue strategies that will survive economic turmoil and continue to attract shrinking individual discretionary dollars will not and cannot be built upon such a view.

Ask. Listen. Look for Insight.

Strategic Principle Two: Innovate

For nonprofits that find themselves increasingly operating in marketlike settings, being open to new ideas for programs or services that respond to changing opportunities is relatively easy. Or, if not easy, the need to do so is at least relatively more compelling. The evidence of failure to be open and creative comes with harsh reality—the market moves resources away from those who do not keep up with innovation.

For other nonprofits, however, there is less of an internal driver toward innovation. Things that have always been done continue to be done because they have been done. So long as loyal supporters will provide money (and sometimes even after supporters themselves have withdrawn that money), interests invested in past ways often hold sway, even when the reality of the operating environment has clearly changed.

This is not simply true of service-providing nonprofits. It can also be true of philanthropy. An example will illustrate the point.

Chapter 3, "Philanthropy within Financial Structures," outlined the demographic changes in the nation. We are aging markedly, and much of the societal commons will increasingly be characterized by the problems and costs of that aging. Questions of health care, ethics, the built environment, economic strain, and family change all now confront the nation, and they will do so with vigor in the near future. Yet, as illustrated in

	Number of Foundations	Number of Grants
Elderly	1,254	31,943
Children/Youth	7,265	181,048

EXHIBIT 8.1 The Focus of Foundation Giving

Exhibit 8.1, the overwhelming focus of the foundation giving remains on children. Indeed, a count of Foundation Center registered grants reveals that foundations make six times as many grants for children's programs as for the elderly. The global survey of high-net-worth individuals jointly conducted in 2009 by Changing Our World and Campden Media found a similar trend. More than 70 percent of respondents felt children's issues were "very important" to their giving (more than 90 percent in North America), while only 21 percent felt the same way about issues of the elderly.[1]

The realities of demographic change and its societal and economic implications appear not to have permeated the perceptions of philanthropies about the needs of the societal commons. This is not a criticism of programming for children, only an illustration of how the aperture of the philanthropic lens has not widened to recognize the changing structure of social need. The argument is not to shift the focus of philanthropy; it is to widen the aperture of its lens to accommodate change.

The same can be said of nonprofits. In April 2009, the *Chronicle of Higher Education* published a fascinating article on universities and the economic crisis.[2] The article points out that the financial crisis of 2008–2009 provides an opportunity for higher education to revisit its entire educational strategy, from the required years of study to the curriculum to the efficiency of administration. Change in the operating environment is an opportunity not a threat. The argument is not that higher education should get into some other line of work. It is that higher education has a perfect chance to use economic crisis to motivate a fundamental reexamination of the way it goes about the business it is in. Regrettably, most institutions of higher education are not seizing that opportunity.

Revenue strategies that are robust in the face of economic scarcity must be premised on an institutional culture that values new ideas and new approaches. True, innovation must be consistent with, and loyally serve, core mission. But the ability to be flexible to new thinking from outside as well as within the organization—to demonstrate continued commitment to a changed community, to widen the aperture of the lens—is an essential prerequisite to revenue strategy that seeks to seize and execute on creative approaches to resource mobilization.

Changing the Focus from Dollars Raised to Community Impact

United Way's access to corporate America is the envy of many nonprofits. Truth be told, while we enjoy strong relationships with many Fortune 500 companies, the traditional model of the CEO-driven workplace campaign—in which United Way shows up once a year to ask for donations and then quickly exits—no longer fulfills the needs of our corporate partners, their employees, or United Way. The value we bring to companies must go well beyond collecting and distributing funds to local health and human service agencies. We must provide our corporate partners with opportunities to actively engage with us over a multiyear period to make a substantial impact on community issues of mutual concern—the quality of education, the financial stability of low-income families, and the elimination of preventable and costly diseases. We must harness the skills, talents, and intellectual capital of their employees in meaningful ways to help produce clear and concrete results in the chosen impact area. And we must report back regularly to tell companies and their employees how their investment in and involvement with United Way is making a difference for individuals and at the community-wide level.

By leveraging our respective assets, we create a win-win situation and change the paradigm from a focus on dollars raised to a focus on community impact. This requires us to think and organize ourselves in new ways. In a real sense, this is one aspect of our revenue diversification. We now seek to cultivate and maintain dynamic relationships with people at all levels within the company—and with individuals throughout our community. Of course, we hope that their experience with United Way year-round will lead to greater loyalty and eventually larger gifts, even after they have left the company for another job or retirement.

Gordon Campbell
President and CEO
United Way of New York City

If that permeability is newly found because an economic speed bump has created organizational crisis—if it is reactive to panic—it will be insufficient. Openness must not be grudging or reactive. If it is, it will be superficial, short-lived, and, ultimately, futile. (See Strategic Principle Five: Know Yourself.) Rather, permeability and innovation must imbue an organization as a central principle so that, at the moment of economic challenge, the foundation for revenue strategy is both firm and flexible. Nonprofit leaders must constantly challenge themselves to innovate based on a continuous awareness of new approaches and new ideas.

When economic times turn harsh, however, the lack of permeability to new ideas and new circumstances is strategically crippling. In his 2000 Letter to Shareholders, Jack Welch, then head of GE, opened his review of the company's progress with the following observation:

> We have long believed that when the rate of change inside an institution becomes slower than the rate of change outside, the end is in sight. It is only a question of when.[3]

Welch is correct. The future will bring constant need for flexibility. Innovation, entrepreneurship, and flexibility are a necessity if institutions are to anticipate, accommodate, and capitalize on changes in their operating environment. The environment will be unforgiving to those institutions that resist change.

Widen the Aperture of the Lens. Be Open to All Ideas. Innovate.

Strategic Principle Three: Expect and Accept Nothing Less than Excellence

Excellence requires hard work, not just hard work internally in an organization's programs and services, but hard work externally, trying to understand the perception of the people and communicate, at every turn and in ways that resonate with people, the importance and quality of what you do.

Chapter 3 has shown that there is a fundamental unease in public opinion about the nonprofit sector. The doubt that accompanied mistakes after the terrorist attacks of September 11, 2001, has never fully ebbed. People doubt that nonprofits spend their money well, and nearly a third of those interviewed believe that the sector is "on the wrong track," as noted in Exhibit 8.2.

The lingering skepticism is perhaps unjust. The nonprofit sector, in the vast majority of its work and for the vast majority of its organizations, performs yeoman's work on the societal commons, in good times and in bad

Leadership and Change

Leadership is changing dramatically. Leaders today need to be more adaptable than ever before. As Xerox CEO Anne Mulcahy says, you can't predict the future. Change comes faster and from more disparate places. So you need to be flexible. And you need to hire people who are good at adapting.

Leaders need to be more empathetic than ever. Empathy is the capacity to see things as others do. Consider Detroit's myopic auto executives, Wall Street's clueless CEOs, and other titans of industry who have stirred populist wrath. Many have fallen because they've failed to understand how their actions—their planes, their perks, their outsized bonuses—play in the public sphere. The best leaders see themselves as others do and don't fall into that trap.

Leaders must be more decisive than ever. Jeff Immelt, the CEO of General Electric, evaluates his managers on five criteria: (1) inclusiveness, (2) imagination/courage, (3) expertise, (4) external focus, and (5) clear thinking/decisiveness. The most difficult to achieve, Immelt told me—for himself and others, typically—is clear thinking/decisiveness. I agree. So many accomplished leaders have told me that their big mistakes have come not from taking a certain action, but rather from not acting quickly enough.

Leaders need to rethink power and their own careers. The best leaders are the ones who define power broadly. They believe that a successful career is not about climbing the ladder. Indeed, if you focus on the next rungs up, how are you going to see the opportunities off to the side? Especially today, when the outlook is uncertain and you don't know what will be the good opportunity tomorrow, a career should be a jungle gym, not a ladder. The most successful leaders tend to swing to opportunities, sometimes lateral, that broaden them.

And I've found: Women, more than men, think about power horizontally. PepsiCo CEO Indra Nooyi talks about "profits with purpose." My favorite definition of power is what Oprah Winfrey told me when I asked her to define the word years ago: "Power is the ability to impact with purpose."

And one more essential leadership trait: communication. You can't be a leader if you don't coax the followers to walk behind you. On on!

Pattie Sellers
Editor at Large
FORTUNE
Chair, Most Powerful Women Summit

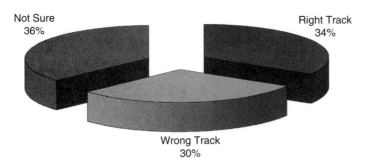

EXHIBIT 8.2 In What Direction Do You Think the Nonprofit Sector Is Going?
Source: Gallup Organization, 2008.

times. Nevertheless, public skepticism is the harsh reality. The only cure is to insist on and demonstrate excellence. This principle extends not just to programs and services, but to core management, financial accountability, and organizational transparency. It is common for organizations to point to evaluations of their services as evidence of their quality. This is important and essential. Unfortunately, the skepticism is not just about services. It is about core organizational competency. A significant portion of people simply do not believe that nonprofits are well managed and transparent with their finances.

The sector has provided, perhaps unwittingly, fuel for that skepticism. It is the rare nonprofit that opens its books to the public. Web sites contain multitudes of pictures and anecdotes about the seriousness of problems and the good that is done in addressing them. Unfortunately, few Web sites also include full copies of audited financials and annual reports that include financial statements. A 2005 survey by Johns Hopkins University found that while 95 percent of nonprofits regularly distribute financial statements to their boards of directors, only 54 percent publish financial statements in their annual reports. Further, only 9 percent posted financial statements on their Web sites.[4] The skeptical public, whose first action increasingly is a click to a Web site, does not find comfort in that absence.

Similarly, few Web sites contain background on the skills of the nonprofit board, the capacities for oversight that are embedded in personal backgrounds. Nor do most Web sites describe the managerial capacity and experience of key executives. There is no question that emphasis on mission and achievements is important. But with 1.2 million public charities in the nation, and chronic public skepticism, revenue strategies will only be effective if they are built on clear managerial excellence and on complete transparency.

Even the most creative revenue strategies for hard times will run aground on the shoals of skepticism unless excellence and transparency is the fundamental platform of an organization's management and programs.

> Open Up the Books and the Biographies. Get Out of the Office and Be with the People.

Strategic Principle Four: Passion Matters but So Do Skills

Matthew Bishop, who coined the term "philanthrocapitalism," has written that the next wave of philanthropic interest will not be about creating new institutions but about "improving the workings of established charitable institutions."[5] The problem with building improvement and sophistication into a revenue strategy is that much in a nonprofit turns on human resources.

No revenue strategy will be successful unless the staff of the organization has two characteristics. First, their own commitment to the organization, their passion for the mission, and their dedication to the work must permeate the spirit of the nonprofit. Strategy can be developed based on philanthropic opportunity, but it has to be executed with vigor by people. An organization without enthusiastic, dedicated staff, managers, and board cannot change, evolve, and improve. All three processes are painful, and it is only dedication that will motivate the willingness to endure the pain. The status quo is comfortable. If optimal strategy calls for overturning the status quo, then the only hope for execution is in the organization with dedicated, hungry staff who want excellence, revenue diversification, and self-reliance more than they want comfort.

Second, the team must have the appropriate skills. This is a huge problem in the nonprofit sector as the nature of philanthropy is redefined. In general, nonprofits lack staff or managers who understand or have experience with complex financing arrangements. It is difficult to take advantage of the emerging complexities embedded in philanthropic flows if no one in the organization is experienced in finance.

Most "nonprofit management" training programs in universities do not include finance in their curricula, for example. "Equity" is a topic in the discussion of ethics and mission, not in the discussion of money. As one moves through the arc of revenue innovation outlined in Chapter 7, "A Systems Approach to Revenue Strategy," nonprofit managers and decision makers need to be exceedingly comfortable with financial analysis. Revenue strategy innovation can be all the more tempting when it is poorly understood. Nonprofits must build strategy on knowledge and skills. The more complex the desired strategy, the more a deep skill base is a fundamental prerequisite for success.

Constantly Build Skills.

Strategic Principle Five: Know Yourself

As noted in Chapter 7, different strategic components of revenue diversification have different conditionality. Therefore, all strategy discussion must be premised on institutional comfort with the conditions likely to be imposed along the revenue arc. This means that all institutions must understand and either know and accept the limits of their own propensity for risk and change or be confident in and committed to the institutional change (and even transformation) that will be necessary to execute complex strategies.

Strategy must be based on an honest institutional assessment of organizational flexibility, acceptance of risk, openness to innovation, and willingness to partner with new types of partners under conditions of negotiation and compromise. If it is not, it will ultimately be a pointless exercise.

One should not minimize the difficultly inherent in this strategic principle. It is as hard to be honest about your organization as it is to be honest about yourself. Indeed, facing such knowledge is harder than implementing change itself.

It is important to accept that organizational assessment must be fact-based. The assessment must not be normative—what a manager or leader thinks *should* be the case—but empirical—what, in fact, *is* the case. When the empirical diverges from the normative—when what is, in fact, the case diverges from what one wishes were the case—the key issue is whether an organization has the will to change. Imposing change on, or expecting change from, an organization whose board, volunteer leaders, managers, and staff do not have the will to change is a painful, often fruitless endeavor. Huge amounts of time and resources are wasted by organizations trying to reach far, far beyond their willingness to make the organizational changes that such an extended grasp would entail. Before embarking on aggressive revenue diversification strategies, therefore, it is an absolute prerequisite that a nonprofit take an honest look at itself, determine its appetite for the changes that will be necessary, and scale the innovation accordingly.

Nonprofits worried about revenues often believe that the resource capacity to invest in revenue diversification is the most critical issue in strategy development. This is not true. The ability to invest in making changes

is not the first question. The will to change—the appetite for innovation—is
the first and priority question.

> Know Yourself.

Notes

1. S. Raymond, B. Love, J. Moore. *Giving Through Generations: Demanding Impact,
   Building Unity, Securing Legacy* (London: Campden Media, March 2009).

2. G. Blumenstyk, "In a Time of Crisis, Colleges Ought to Be Making History,"
   Chronicle of Higher Education, May 1, 2009, 1.

3. Annual Report to Shareholders, General Electric Corporation, 2000.

4. "Nonprofit Governance and Accountability," Johns Hopkins Nonprofit Listening
   Post Project, October 2005.

5. M. Bishop, "Philanthrocapitalism on Trial," *Chronicle on Philanthropy (2007)*,
   21:2, 30.

CHAPTER 9

Getting Down to Specifics
Strategy for Complexity

The heights by great men reached and kept / Were not attained by sudden flight, / But they, while their companions slept, / Were toiling upward in the night.

"The Ladder of St. Augustine"

Henry Wadsworth Longfellow

Understanding Movement within the Analytic Framework

Diversifying from the "pure giving—pure nonprofit" at the bottom left of the framework of analysis (see Exhibit 7.2) toward more complex financing options does not mean replacing one method with another. Alternatives are not mutually exclusive; they build forward as appropriate. A strategy that seeks to develop social enterprise options may not supplant strategy that deepens and increases expressive philanthropy. The overall need, based on the common elements in Chapter 8, "Common Principles for Robust Strategy," is for strategy that appropriately strengthens core financing capacity and creates the human and the organizational capacity to build out other, diverse options within the willingness and ability of an organization to accept narrower conditions on those funds.

Thematic Summary

Diversifying revenue by moving along the analytic framework requires strategy within each dimension as well as overcoming organizational and cultural barriers to transitioning between the dimensions. Not all

(Continued)

> (*Continued*)
> options are for all organizations. Neither does movement toward more market-driven options replace solicitation of pure philanthropy. However, as more complexity comes with more diversity, the management demands of strategy also increase, and smaller organizations will have increasingly greater difficulty with additional diversity. This can become the thorn in the side of the nonprofit sector in economic hard times. The smallest and perhaps most frail organizations, which are also the most vulnerable, may have the greatest difficulty mastering the very diversity that could be their strength.

Therefore, we proceed to discuss diversification strategy in four parts. We begin with the strategy to deepen and broaden the commitments of expressive philanthropy to the core mission of a nonprofit. Second, we move on to strategies that allow a build out from this platform to philanthropy that, while still having the characteristics of a "gift," is additionally encumbered with conditions that impose added expectations or limits on the traditional nonprofit. Third, we "cross the line" of the first boundary to capacity transition, taking revenue diversification into Strategy Area B, where the revenue takes on many of the characteristics of competitive markets and return on investment. Finally, we cross the second capacity line to discuss strategies for more complex revenue options that are directly derived from, or directly operate via, commercial markets.

Again, it is important to realize that the progression through the framework of analysis is additive. Multiple strategies can be sequenced to lead to diversification. To illustrate this point, a hypothetical case is gradually built throughout this chapter, to indicate how a relatively straightforward nonprofit with a relatively pure giving base, in this case a soup kitchen, could evolve to diversify its revenue base, and the prerequisites and organizational adjustments necessary for it to do so. The illustration is not based on any single institution but represents an amalgam of experiences of nonprofits and quasi-nonprofits as they move through the revenue diversification process.

Before beginning, a final word on budgets is important. Movement along the strategy framework requires resources. Crossing each capacity barrier requires changes and an investment in new skills and systems. These resources must come from reorienting budgets or from new grants to support strategy evolution. Revenue diversification is a constant process, and the resources to enable it must be consciously budgeted internally or sought externally.

Expressive Philanthropy: Strategy Base = Communicating Shared Values

Traditional expressive philanthropy represents a flow of funds largely on the basis of shared vision or shared values between nonprofit and donor. The essential base for strategy is the fundamental and largely unconditional nature of that relationship. Donors ask for little in return, except the knowledge that the nonprofit is engaged in the good works that both donor and nonprofit value. (See Exhibit 9.1.)

History and economic challenge teach one rule: Never be complacent. The only way to prepare for the revenue challenges of economic downturns when operating in the expressive philanthropy space is to live life on your toes. The combination of 1.2 million nonprofits, falling household income and rising unemployment, and hundreds of worthy causes means that strategy for hard times must be ever poised to adjust to opportunity. In the face of economic challenge, there is a temptation to withdraw, to hunker down, to wait for better times. This is a fatal error. Strategy for hard times must build on fundamental strengths and be proactive, identifying and seeking

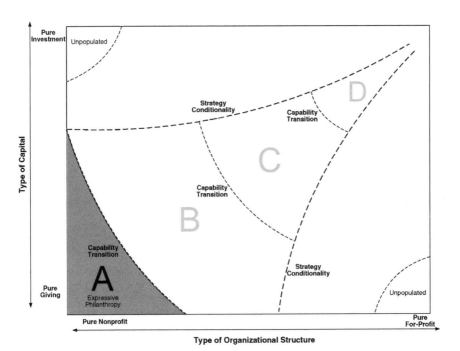

EXHIBIT 9.1 Strategy Area A: Expressive Philanthropy

out new audiences for support, new programs to inaugurate, and new ways to cement the engagement of traditional supporters. Withdrawal, in effect, cedes the philanthropic space to others.

The fundamental components of strategy are fivefold. Although the components are cast here in terms of nonprofits, many of the same principles apply to philanthropies in preparing for operations during inevitable economic downturns.

Strategy for Hard Times Must Be Set in Good Times

All healthy economies are cyclic. When the lengthy and in many ways historic recession of 2008–2009 is relegated to the classroom, one thing will be certain. Another economic downturn will occur. Preparing for that certainty before it becomes reality is essential to avoid strategy set in panic. Panic is not conducive to wise or productive decision making. Surprise is never a good thing.

Therefore, managers, boards of directors, and development directors must take three steps in good times. First, develop a clear set of early-warning indicators that will enable the nonprofit to anticipate approaching problems with enough time to trigger successful action. This would include changes in revenue, of course, but also might include changes in board-giving behavior, changes in job markets, and subtle but persistent changes in the demand pattern for the nonprofit's services. Formal responsibility should be given to an individual within the organization for tracking these indicators and reporting regularly to management and board on their trends. Information is the key to anticipation.

Second, the nonprofit should develop a game plan for a downturn. Study and learn from past experience. Make decisions in good times about the choices that will be needed in hard times. Where will continued investment be necessary; what will need to be pared back; what will need to be undertaken to ensure continued philanthropic inflows? That game should be reviewed regularly, perhaps every two years, to ensure that it remains current relative to the nonprofit's programs and philanthropic support.

Third, develop a contingency budget. Know what the financial dimensions of action will be and understand the budgeting choices that will be needed. Determine how and when those choices will be made. Again, review that preparation periodically to ensure that the information and analysis is current. If surprise is never a good thing, budgetary surprise inflicts the most pain and, often, results in disinvestment in precisely the areas thought in panic to be expendable (e.g., communications), which are, in fact, most critical in hard times. Think through budgetary priorities outside of the crucible of economic distress.

The Evolution of Revenue Diversification

A Hypothetical Case of the Oak Street Soup Kitchen of Rivertown

The following hypothetical case study tracks an illustrative nonprofit's organizational change as it seeks to align its mission with a changing environment and with changing opportunities. Any similarity to any existing institution is totally coincidental.

Part I: The Beginnings

Nearly 80 years ago, in the depths of the Great Depression, a group of five stalwart citizens of Rivertown founded the Oak Street Soup Kitchen. Originally operated out of the garage of one of the founders, the kitchen provided a hot lunch to anyone in need. Word spread, and as the numbers grew, so did the generosity of the people of Rivertown. Millers donated day-old bread, farmers—even those who faced loss of their farms—brought in damaged vegetables for the soup, children collected pennies. It seemed, at times, that the entire community stood should-to-shoulder with the soup kitchen and those most deeply affected by the Depression.

In a matter of months, the Oak Street Church cleared the north end of its basement, the town issued an occupancy permit, and the soup kitchen moved from the garage into the church basement. Still the contributions came, often just in time to save "the Kitchen," as it became known, from having to turn away the poor. And the Depression dragged on. And on. And on. Day after day, month after month, the citizens of Rivertown volunteered and donated to prevent those worst affected from hunger. The Kitchen and the community became one in spirit.

Gradually, times changed. The economy improved. The lines of the hungry slowly decreased. Yet, the problem never really went away—indeed perhaps it had always existed, even before the Kitchen was founded, but was just never recognized. In any event, the Kitchen became a local charitable institution and a formal registered tax exempt public charity. It created a board of directors, but the staff remained an "all volunteer force." Indeed, there were often more volunteers than work to do. The Kitchen was a point of local pride.

Susan Raymond, Ph.D.
Executive Vice President
Changing Our World, Inc.

Expand the Volunteer Corps

The successful nonprofit must embed its community of supporters through-out its operations. During hard times, develop new mechanisms for doing just that. Develop new jobs and new roles for volunteers. Develop entirely new approaches to volunteerism.

Economic hard times are not just hard for nonprofits; they are hard for people, too. Unemployment may mean that more people are available to help at service sites. But it may also mean that more people are working multiple jobs to make ends meet. Understand the structure of the impact of economic downturn on individuals and families. Consider ways to allow volunteers to contribute valuable services even from their homes. Are there envelopes to be stuffed? Lists to be culled? Ways in which needs can be Web-based, and hence volunteers assist through electronic means? Can people be engaged at their convenience, whenever that is, not at the convenience of the nonprofit? Make the central volunteer principle be ease for the volunteers not ease for the nonprofit.

Expanding the volunteer corps, in terms that volunteers can accommo-date, has two subsidiary benefits beyond assisting with the service capacity of a nonprofit. First, it allows people to see for themselves the increased demand being placed on nonprofit services in hard times. It presses home the value of the nonprofit in its community. Second, it can begin to establish loyalties with new cohorts of community members who will then become philanthropic sources when the economy rebounds. Use hard times to reach out to new supporters through expanded volunteer efforts. Those who volunteer are more likely to contribute to the organizations to which they have committed their time. Knowledge and closer engagement earned during hard times will pay dividends in the future.

Restructure and Renew Leadership

Because creative economic destruction provides opportunity for commercial and technological change, an economic downturn provides an equal oppor-tunity for reassessment of leadership. In economic crisis, many nonprofits look to their boards in desperation, hoping that financial salvation will come, in part, from renewed board financial commitment. This is often the case. But it is an insufficient optic through which to view board leadership in trying times. Nonprofit management needs to become well-versed not sim-ply in the economic crisis of the moment, but in the details of the likely climb out. What industries will strengthen? Which will weaken? What tech-nologies will lead? What geographic locations—including globally—have retained strength, and which will lead a recovery?

Anticipating these trends can help identify pools of leadership to be recruited to boards even as an economy languishes. Indeed, it is in that period of economic quiescence that such leaders should be cultivated. Once an economy rebounds, it is often difficult to attract the time and attention of leaders who are, once again, enmeshed in 20-hour days, 7 days a week on four continents. Analyze the board relative to the likely nature of the economic recovery, and cultivate tomorrow's leadership.

For many nonprofit managers, this is a difficult strategic prescription. Their networks can be narrow and largely set by the existing board. Publications, Web sites, and professional materials in the nonprofit sector are exceedingly inward looking. This is particularly true in an economic downturn, when virtually all of the media eyes within the sector turn toward documenting the trials and tribulations of the sector itself. By and large, publications within the nonprofit and philanthropic sector do not analyze the likely economic or industrial nature of an economic recovery from recession, or the fund-raising or philanthropic implications of the changes in the basic structure and functioning of the economy that would likely ensue. Nonprofit managers are unlikely to obtain guidance or insight on these fundamental dimensions of a changed economic operating environment from analysis inside the nonprofit sector itself.

Managers will have to turn elsewhere. Read the *Wall Street Journal,* the *Financial Times, Forbes, Fortune,* and any other local economic and business journals available. Cull them for trends, innovations, names, and alignments with your nonprofit's mission, needs, or existing board networks. Ensure that every board meeting includes an agenda item on the economy in two parts, the problems currently faced and the nature of, and philanthropic opportunities possible within, the recovery.

Reassess and Refresh Programs

When times are good, nonprofits often have neither the energy (nor, in some cases, the motivation) to reassess their programs relative to a changing operating environment. Things are going well; donations are coming in; services are being provided; cruise control is engaged.

The disruption of economic hard times often is a shock to the system of nonprofit finance and management. It should also be used as a purposeful shock to the system of programs. Disruption is a perfect opportunity to completely reassess a nonprofit's program environment, including changing demographics in the service area, changing income structure, or changing client needs or preferences. That assessment must be forward-looking. In times of change, it does little good to know the world of today. It is the world of tomorrow that matters. The operating environment assessment should look at least 10 years into the future to anticipate the direction and implications of today's changes.

This assessment should form the base for an evaluation of the organization's entire service portfolio. That evaluation should be followed by appropriate program redesign. In turn, the updating of program approaches, targets, and content then becomes the base for articulation of the strategic direction of the nonprofit as the economy recovers.

In addition to ensuring that a nonprofit's services constantly reflect the pulse of change (in and of itself, a necessary characteristic of organizational excellence), there are several strategic advantages to this approach. First, it provides a refreshed organizational profile on which discussions with new leaders can take place. The nonprofit is positioned not simply as supplicant to new leaders, but as a renewed organization.

Second, it opens the way for reassessing philanthropy sources. Innovations based on a changing environment may suggest new alignments with different sources of funds than have been traditionally approached. If a service population is changing its demography, for example, program adjustments to that reality will open up new philanthropies interested in the characteristics of the altered demographic. This becomes part of the three-year plan discussed below.

Third, even for existing supporters, reassessment positions the nonprofit as being in tune with changing community. It reinforces the image of an organization that, even in times of challenge, is not in panic, is not complacent, is not in hiding. Rather, it reflects an organization that is so committed to community that, even under stress, it is adapting to change so that it can serve community better.

Develop an Institution-Wide Three-Year Philanthropic Plan

Most nonprofits understand that any hope of philanthropic stability requires multiyear fund-raising planning. Faced with economic crisis, many of these same organizations cease planning. The pressure of the urgent crowds out the priority of the important. This is both understandable and unfortunate.

Strategy to recover and grow requires a clear revenue plan, in the case of philanthropy, a clear fund-raising plan. That plan must build on the four strategic components above. It must capitalize on expanded volunteer efforts, take advantage of likely new leadership, and draw on refreshed program approaches to identify new support sources. It must use economic difficulties to build a plan for broadening the base of organizational support across larger numbers of people whose gifts may be smaller, and at the same time prepare for overtures to larger donors as economic recovery picks up steam.

What is critical in periods of economic challenge is that the philanthropic plan be unlike any other in two aspects.

First, it must be geared to the pace and nature of the economic recovery. Tactics in plan need to be sequenced to rebuilding of the muscle within an economy. This requires that management and boards, tracking economic trends for leadership assessment, be deeply embedded in the philanthropic plan itself. In turn, those in fund development must be deeply embedded in the economic discussion accompanying leadership renewal.

Second, if it is to be effective, a three-year plan that is geared to an economic climb out cannot be the product solely of the development department. It must be the product of the entire decision-making structure of the nonprofit. Economic hard times require all nonprofits to tear down their internal silos and develop a philanthropic plan that capitalizes on all opportunities identified anywhere in the organization, from the board outward to every service program. Knowledge, intelligence, and ideas must be drawn from all other work to build a robust climb-out plan.

Economic crisis is not the time to suspend forward-looking philanthropic planning. It is the opportunity to position an organization on the track, firmly set in the running blocks at the starting line, with a strategy that sequences tactics to growing opportunity.

Rising Expectations: Strategy Base = Evidence and Interest Alignment

As one moves to expand strategy into other forms of philanthropy and ultimately into marketlike revenue mechanisms, the strategy playing field begins to narrow. Conditionality begins to limit approaches and options. Not all organizations can or should overcome the challenges inherent in that movement. For those that do, barriers must be faced and strategy takes on a new dimension that must accommodate donor expectations and interests. (See Exhibit 9.2.)

The central theme in strategy for expressive philanthropy is relationships based on shared values. Moving along the analytic framework from pure expressive philanthropy to more diverse revenue from giving that is contingent on factors other than shared values must overcome barriers to that transition. These have been discussed throughout this book. To reprise, there are four impediments that any nonprofit must overcome in moving into Strategy Area B of the revenue diversification analytic framework that is often premised less on the nonprofits mission than on the needs/views/interests of the organization providing the funds.

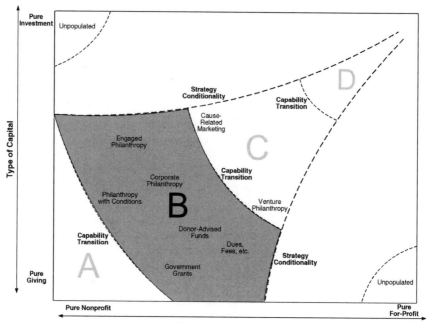

EXHIBIT 9.2 Strategy Area B: Expectations Increase

First, expertise is often a prerequisite. Donors who are interested in evidence expect nonprofits to produce quantitative data. Many nonprofits, especially those that are small, do not have the internal staff expertise to produce such data.

Second, knowledge of the specific conditions and specific expectations of funders is also essential. This extends both to private philanthropies and to government sources of funds. This knowledge requires staff or managers with broad exposure and networks, who know that funders actually want compared to what they say they want. The knowledge barrier is not so much information as it is intelligence, the deeper meaning and expectations embedded in information.

Third, crossing the transition barrier requires internal systems for tracking outcome/impact information over time, for developing complex proposals, and for managing the ongoing peer relations that often are required between funders and grantees when funders see themselves as more than mere check writers. Systems are the lubricants that make the gears of evidence-based philanthropy run smoothly.

Fourth, the capability transition is often blocked by the need for flexibility. Evidence/interest-based philanthropy often requires the nonprofit to meet the funder on some middle ground. The corporate grant maker may want alignment with corporate products and goals. The engaged philanthropist may want his or her own personal involvement in program development. The government agency may premise funding on execution of its own policy interests. The foundation may wish programs to be evaluated on its own terms. All require the nonprofit to hold to mission and to be flexible about its own systems, programs, and approaches. For many nonprofits, this is often the barrier that is hardest to cross in diversifying away from the purely altruistic provision of funds on the basis of shared values to the more conditional provision of funds on the basis of funder expectations and interests. There is no right or wrong nonprofit response. But inflexibility effectively bars diversification of revenue into Area B of the analytic framework.

Key components to strategy for those who can cross the transition barrier are several-fold.

Build Full and Complete Internal Communication

Because so much of what is expected by donors in Strategy Area B is premised on and directed to programs, it is critical that the diversifying nonprofit establish deep communication between programs offices and development/finance offices. Fund-raising is no longer simply about a compelling case and a dedication to mission. Grants flow to program rigor and evidence of impact. Moreover, supporters may want personal engagement and deep organizational involvement. Development offices do not control program content or execution. Neither can they promise program involvement. If deep cooperation between development professionals and program professionals is not forged, internal strife is certain to follow.

Revenue diversification strategy that moves into Strategy Area B must begin with a clear model for internal communication and cooperation, and a clear system for funding responsibility and accountability. Promises that must be made to donors must be able to be kept and, equally, must be seen as value-added, not as burdens, by those responsible for program service execution.

Invest in an Evidence Culture

Because so much of Area B is premised on evidence, a critical element of revenue strategy is the willingness and ability to invest in internal systems of data collection and measurement. This requires more than human resources, although expertise is important. It requires that institutions from boards through management and into program staff understand, accept, and even embrace the degree to which programs and services will need to

The Evolution of Revenue Diversification

A Hypothetical Case of the Oak Street Soup Kitchen of Rivertown

Part II: Years of Change

By the 1980s, with the national emphasis on private rather than government solutions to local problems, the Kitchen's board decided to apply for government-subsidized food and begin a food pantry as well, providing staples and nonperishable canned food to those in need. This required coordination with the local social welfare department, various inspections and permits, a full-time executive director, and an accounting system. The Kitchen had never had more than $25,000 in cash income, since most soup material was donated, so it had never filed formal Form 990s with the IRS.

The board determined that the advantages of growth outweighed the costs of change. The population of Rivertown had tripled since 1950, including the recent influx of immigrants from around the world. The income structure of Rivertown was changing, and the portion of the residents who were low-income or fixed-income elderly was growing. Needs were becoming more obvious, and the influx of subsidized food would enable the Kitchen to grow with them.

With a change and formalization of its structure and a professionalization of two staff positions, the Kitchen not only served more people but incurred greater fixed costs. Although local financial contributions continued, the combination of growing demand for services and the increased number of formal foundations in the area resulted in the board's awareness that there was a need for more resources and an opportunity to reach into new philanthropic sources to obtain those resources.

In 1990, the board and executive director decided to expand fundraising into two new areas. Although the charity of local loyal donors would continue to be sought, an aggressive effort would be made to acquire large grants from foundations, and greater effort would be made to find corporate supporters. In short order, the difficulty was made clear.

Foundations expected the Kitchen to be able to demonstrate not just its succor to the poor, but the degree of its effectiveness in addressing their needs. "Cups of soup served" was assumed to be the method by which the kitchen pursued its mission. But "cups of soup served" was not an acceptable goal. The kitchen needed to demonstrate that it was making a material difference in eliminating the need for serving cups of soup to begin with. So the Kitchen realigned itself. It hired a social worker, developed closer relationships with the municipal department of social services, negotiated a partnership with two nonprofits, one providing transitional housing and the other providing job training services. Those who came to the Kitchen were not simply served; they were assessed and referred to more comprehensive service providers. The Kitchen developed a database of its clients, tracking referrals and regularly following up to measure recurrent service, effectiveness of referrals, and ultimately income and social self-reliance.

Over five years, the social service staff payroll at the Kitchen tripled, and the Kitchen found it necessary to contract with a freelance Ph.D. evaluation specialist to develop the tools to produce the data required by foundation supporters. The Kitchen added to its board two academics from the local university. Foundation fund-raising was successful, and that payroll was met. But every quarter, the operations costs of the Kitchen required more and more attention to aggressive acquisition of large foundation grants to ensure financial viability. This effort also required the allocation of increased amounts of the executive director's time in overseeing impact reporting and visiting with multiple foundation staff who increasingly wished to be involved in programmatic decisions.

The corporate strategy entailed equal challenges and associated changes. Most Rivertown companies had long supported the Kitchen with small grants. One of the most loyal supporters over 30 years had been Rivertown Millers, a family-owned company that had long been the mainstay not only of the Rivertown economy, but also of its social and charitable structures. Economic change had arrived at the doorstep of the company, however. Rivertown Millers had just been acquired by Coast-to-Coast Foods (CCF), a Fortune 100 multinational food and beverage company. When the Kitchen approached Rivertown Millers with a request for an unprecedented $1 million grant to expand its operations and seed an endowment to stabilize the ability to meet the more complex payroll, Rivertown Millers's management referred the matter to its new top managers. CCF soon sent a delegation to the Kitchen, composed of a staff member of its corporate foundation and a junior member of its marketing department.

CCF had deep social responsibility roots and a national reputation as a corporate citizen. But strengthened markets for boutique organic foods and rising consumer criticism of multinational trading practices for basic commodities in the developing world was leading CCF to look for ways to align its corporate social responsibility and philanthropy programs more closely with its corporate messaging. That messaging emphasized not just its commitment to doing good, but the relationship

(Continued)

(*Continued*)

between its business and the good that was done. The CCF delegation was intrigued with the history and community roots of the Kitchen as emblematic of both local charity and the positive role that food could play in poverty alleviation.

Initial discussions with staff of the Kitchen were tense. Compromises with large foundations were pulling the Kitchen toward a diversification of programming to achieve diversification of revenue. CCF's desire for stronger message alignment in exchange for a large financial commitment would pull the Kitchen back to its previous food-only history but, it became clear, involve an alignment between the Kitchen and CCF's brand. Two staff members resigned even before an agreement was reached. The resignations were covered in the local press, and the lead editorial deplored "the meddling of big agro-business in the soul of this community's sacred solidarity with the needs of its own poor."

Yet the managers and employees of Rivertown Millers implored the Kitchen to work with CCF. Employees had long been loyal volunteers at the Kitchen, and Rivertown Millers commitment to the Kitchen was a major point of pride among employees and one of its greatest assets in recruiting midlevel managers to what otherwise would have been seen as just another food company in the nation's heartland. Ultimately, the board of the Kitchen met with CCF representatives and developed a strategy that included a five-year grant commitment and a onetime $1 million lead grant to its fledgling endowment. In exchange, the Kitchen would recognize CCF prominently on its Web site, allow CCF to include a profile of its commitment to the Kitchen in its annual report, and give the president of Rivertown Millers a board seat for a normal two-year rotation, but indicating that Rivertown was a CCF subsidiary.

be evidence-oriented. For many nonprofits, this growing emphasis creates discomfort and a fear that it supplants mission. Efforts to satisfy evidence-based donors, then, become reluctant or superficial and create consequent frustration and disillusionment for both funder and nonprofit.

The investment strategy must be in the skills and systems capable of tracking and producing evidence of programmatic results. It must also be in developing and embracing an organizational culture that sees evidence as part of the DNA of the nonprofit's work.

Establish Basic Compromise Criteria

As noted earlier, Strategy Area B is likely to entail some degree of organizational compromise. The pull for responsiveness to the specific interests of diverse companies, agencies, or philanthropists will come from many directions. Openness to donors' interests and ideas is an important prerequisite to revenue strategy in Area B. However, the absolute worst thing any nonprofit can do is chase every diverse dollar by promising to adjust to every diverse demand. Frantic efforts in economic hard times to fit organization and program to multiple conflicting expectations of engaged donors is a recipe for disillusionment on the part of both the nonprofit and its supporters. The nonprofit will quickly lose its way, erode its identity, and probably find its best personnel heading for the exits. The supporting agency or philanthropy will be disillusioned that promises are not met and organizational capacity erodes.

A key element of strategy, then, is to determine precisely how the organization will engage supporters in Strategy Area B. It is important the program executives, senior managers, and board members consider in advance their willingness/ability to undertake program adjustments, add program innovations, or measure and evaluate in ways that are outside the organizational norm.

Too often, nonprofits assume that accommodation can be made on an ad hoc basis. The result is often confusion and resentment. Overtures are made and initial discussions undertaken. As those discussions proceed, it becomes clear, for example, that a corporation actually expects to align its cause-related marketing with its markets—indeed, that is why it engages in the effort to begin with. The nonprofit gradually (or not so gradually) comes to realize that those market desires are orthogonal to its own priorities. Suddenly, the nonprofit begins to pull back or complicate the dialogue as it struggles with how to align. The funder becomes frustrated with the confusion. The relationship erodes and withers or explodes.

If a nonprofit has not already anticipated and decided how it will approach accommodating a donor's own goals and objectives, relationships in Strategy Area B can be exceedingly difficult to structure. A clear understanding about how much flexibility is possible and what skills and adjustments are needed is important to ensuring that new relationships with new types of funders and expectations result in both revenue and organizational strengthening.

Proactively Identify and Articulate Alignments

It is important to realize that successful strategy to develop revenue sources based on evidence of impact and philanthropist engagement is as cultivation-intense as major gifts strategies are in Strategy Area A with pure donor gifts. Successful approaches are only secondarily about proposal writing. There are two key actions that must precede mastery of the word processor.

First, the successful nonprofit must come to be known by the target funding institutions. This requires cultivation of funders on two levels—at the level of programs and at the level of management. Often, companies or foundations or even individual philanthropists in this Strategy Area need to be familiar with and have trust in the technical capacity and human resources of the nonprofit to which they are making an often significant commitment. This is not a matter of the salience of nonprofit's mission; it is a matter of its competence. This is natural; the philanthropy is considered less a gift than an investment, so the question of competence is a driving issue. Trust in that competence takes time and exposure. Program managers will need to take the time and effort to impress (often repeatedly) funders with their work, and to do so in ways that resonate with the goals of the technical staff of the funder. Similarly, executive directors or other top managers will need to invest the time and effort to understand deeply the interests and expectations of donors. Rather than pushing programs to donors, pull donors to programs by articulating competence in terms that align with philanthropist interests. Philanthropists have no lack of choices for nonprofit partners. Executive directors need to invest the time to understand the expectations of the market and not wait for the market to discover their nonprofit.

Second, the plan must be specific and specifically aligned. Donors in Strategy Area B assume good intent and good works. They seek initiatives that align with their predetermined interests and desires for impact. Nonprofits should not expect that donors in this Strategy Area will automatically see the alignment. The onus of responsibility for articulating that alignment, and even demonstrating it with evidence, is on the nonprofit. That demonstration cannot be the product of the grant making; it must precede the overture for funds.

Strategy Area B requires that nonprofits think first not about what they do and what they want, but what the funder is trying to accomplish and how their work serves that end. This is not easy. Nor is it always appropriate. But funder desires and expectations are the drivers for the narrowing of the strategy conditionality boundary that begins to limit nonprofit maneuvering room as nonprofits move from expressive philanthropy to philanthropy that comes with greater and greater contingencies.

Seek Out and Cultivate Collaboration

A central theme of donor expectations in Strategy Area B is that philanthropic investments actually fix problems. Where relationships dominated the nonprofit-philanthropy linkage in Strategy Area A, ongoing support is intended to continue good works. Venture philanthropists, engaged philanthropy, corporate philanthropy, and even, to some extent, government support expects more. The emphasis is not on continued effort; it is on actually solving the targeted problem, or at least demonstrating that the problem can be solved. The premium is accomplishment, and often accomplishment at scale.

Nonprofits seeking to operate in this context should include collaboration in their strategies. Few complex problems rest within in one subject area, and few complex problems can be fully addressed by one organization. When donors are focused on solutions at scale, nonprofits should develop strategies targeted at that focus. In turn, that often requires collaboration among individual nonprofit organizations. Proactive development of cross-organization collaboration can both distinguish the approach to a problem and demonstrate that a group of nonprofits is as committed to problem solving as the engaged or venture philanthropist.

Collaborative strategy requires a combination of creativity and courage. Although collaborating nonprofits do not need to give up their existence, they do often need to give up sole control over the design and execution of initiatives at scale. This is often not an easy task. However, in Strategy Area B, philanthropists are looking for solutions. Self-initiated programmatic collaboration on the part of complementary or synergistic nonprofits, focused on a shared goal with mutual measures of achievement, can provide both a distinguishing characteristic and evidence of commitment of nonprofits to actually solving problems at scale.

Quasi-Markets: Strategy Base = Competitive Self-Reliance

Moving from Strategy Area B to Strategy Area C requires that a nonprofit overcome what can be even higher barriers to strategy development and execution. Revenue strategy in Strategy Area C is premised on quasi-markets. Resource transfers are based on competition and on investment. They are often analogies of commercial strategies for capitalization. Relationships and evidence of impact may be important, but the basis of resource flows is an effort to develop strategies for capital and for operating revenue that will drive toward financial self-reliance for the organization. (See Exhibit 9.3.)

Indeed, for some tools in this area, the line between commercial markets and nonprofit mission blurs. Some adaptations— for example, the development of weather insurance mechanisms to insure against famine in Africa— are purely commercial tools, which, used by a nonprofit, flow resources to mission (restoration of food production capacity among the poor) in nearly commercial terms.

The capability transition barrier for the nonprofit seeking to add strategy in Area C to its revenue arsenal is significant. Such strategies not only require

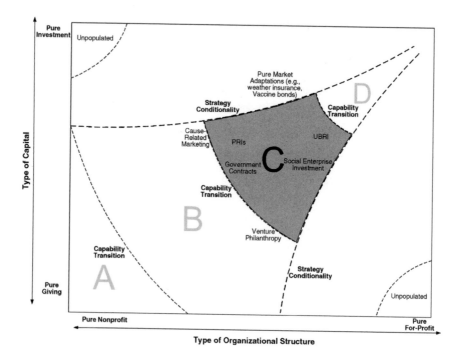

EXHIBIT 9.3 Strategy Area C: Quasi-Markets

entirely new skills, they require deep knowledge about how commercial investment or market instruments work and the ways in which they fit, and do not fit, nonprofit work. They require extreme experience in assessing and managing financial risk, and the capacity to continually assess the financial implications of the strategies for the medium and long term.

Further, in many cases, the strategies may require a nonprofit to think about itself in an entirely different way. It must see itself as an investable enterprise, not as a needy charity. It must see its revenue strategy as a means to building sustained self-reliance, not as a way to fill budget gaps. Strategy, then, is based on what is, in some ways, a different mind-set about organizational development. Crossing into Strategy Area C requires a propensity for seeing the world through entrepreneurial eyes. Where that vision is, or could be made to be, consistent with an organization's culture, there are a series of strategic elements that need to be considered.

Rethink the Board

Many nonprofit boards are composed of individuals deeply committed to organizational mission but not deeply experienced in finance, business

The Evolution of Revenue Diversification

A Hypothetical Case of the Oak Street Soup Kitchen of Rivertown

Part III: Big Decisions

By 2002, more than a decade after they had begun, the diversification strategies had increased and stabilized revenue at the Kitchen. However, the Kitchen gradually noticed that, in the course of that decade, local donations were falling and the average size of donations was declining. It seemed that the effort to diversify, although successful, was crowding out the roots of local commitment. A poll of current and lapsed donors indicated a growing sense of distance, a perception that the Kitchen had grown beyond its local roots and was "someone else's problem."

Simultaneously, that very diversification was under threat. The philosophy of philanthropy nationwide was changing. Innovation became the coin of the realm. The emphasis was not on charity, but on enterprise. How could problems be solved permanently? How could markets be joined with social needs to produce goods and services that addressed social need "markets"?

The executive director of the Kitchen, who had been a volunteer for 10 years before being hired as the first manager and so had been at the helm for more than 20 years, balked at these new concepts. Locally lauded and even lionized as a "selfless saint" by the local press, he had tolerated, but not initiated, the growth and changes that had accompanied revenue strategies in the 1990s. "Enterprise" was not a comfortable (let alone a comforting) concept.

Nevertheless, the growing recognition of the opportunity for linking the Kitchen to self-reliant strategies for clients was "the buzz" among younger volunteers. Between 1980 and 2002, Rivertown College had become Rivertown University. It had founded a new business school, the James School, endowed by and named after the founder of Rivertown Millers. The dean of the business school approached the chair of the Kitchen's board with a new concept. Why not use the Kitchen as a training ground for impoverished youth to develop food service industry skills? The Kitchen could not only expand the number of meals it served but, in the process, provide much needed job training. The chairman was intrigued. The executive director was not.

Over a period of two years, the board chairman and the dean gradually convinced the board of the viability of the concept, discussed the

(Continued)

(Continued)

idea with CCF and the Rivertown Community Foundation, and assigned three third-year business students to develop the business plan for a training program. That business plan also extended the concept to the development of a catering service that would flow earnings to the charitable side of the Kitchen and further diversify and expand its revenue. The key to the catering plan was to produce healthy, attractive, yet nearly gourmet dishes from the same simple, cheap ingredients that the Kitchen used in its everyday services to the needy.

The executive director announced his retirement. With a new leader in place, chosen for her background in organizational innovation, the Kitchen raised the venture philanthropy for the initiative from an anonymous donor to the Community Foundation, and embarked on a social enterprise effort called Foods from the Kitchen (FTK). In the second year of its operation, FTK received a three-year grant from federal government to anchor its budget.

Within five years, FTK was training 25 chefs per year and providing net catering revenue of $750,000 per year to fund the charitable soup kitchen and food pantry. FTK's Three Bean Puffs and its Kale Tofu Surprise were on the party tables of nearly every social event in Rivertown.

The road had not been smooth, however. Several inspections by the Department of Public Health had identified problems in sanitation, one of which required a temporary halt to operations and front-page news coverage.

Still, FTK was the talk of the social enterprise sector, and the Kitchen's executive director was the hit of the speaking circuit. The Kitchen hired a chief operating officer for FTK, a full-time chief financial officer, and an associate executive director for the Kitchen itself.

Donations from community supporters continued to drop. By 2006, donations represented just 15 percent of total revenues. However, the Kitchen tripled its feeding program in the previous decade, expanded its food pantry, and now had a reliable funds balance of $10 million. The Kitchen had comfortably handled the enormous spike in demand during the 2000–2002 recession when unemployment in Rivertown had risen to nearly 8 percent.

planning, or entrepreneurship. Undertaking loan, equity, or social enterprise approaches to revenue diversity requires detailed understanding of both the financial and market alternatives for enterprises so that market-based analogies can be incorporated into revenue diversification without organizational disruption. It is possible to be too clever by half. A skilled board is the best antidote to overreaching in revenue creativity. It is also a critical strategy for reaching new audiences. For example, entrepreneurs often bring access to private banks.

However, board restructuring is not always possible, nor is it always advisable, particularly if commitment to capital and enterprise innovations is tentative or exploratory. In such cases, a skilled advisory committee to the finance committee of the board can serve the purpose of embedding skills in the design and decision-making process without committing board positions to a strategy with uncertain outcomes. Indeed, the advisory committee could become a testing ground for possible new board members, or board restructuring, should enterprise-based experiments prove productive.

Be Purposeful in Obtaining Institution and Community Buy-In

Investment and enterprise innovations, even if they supplement but do not displace existing revenue and program approaches, can be divisive. Individuals resist change; institutions normally have allergic reactions to change. Consideration of revenue diversification into Strategy Area C must be accompanied by intense efforts by managers to educate staff at all levels.

The possible problems, however, do not stop at the doors of the nonprofit itself. Management must also be conscious of the reactions of volunteers and the public. A nonprofit usually has a particular image and reputation in its community. Volunteers usually engage in a nonprofit's mission out of personal interest and experience. Both image and volunteer ranks are years in the making. Exploration of investment or enterprise revenue options, if poorly understood or allowed to spin into rumor, can do significant harm both to image and to the trust and commitment of volunteers. Chapter 4, "Emerging Nonprofit Revenue Parameters," pointed out the degree to which public opinion about nonprofit trustworthiness continues to be problematic in the United States. Complex revenue strategies, poorly understood by supporters and bystanders alike and inevitably covered in the local media, can quickly erode trust.

The views of those whom the nonprofit serves also need to be informed. Surprise is never a good thing, but it is a particularly bad thing when those who are surprised are, themselves, under social or economic stress. The link to image and volunteers is also clear; where volunteers become concerned, they are likely to communicate that concern to those being served.

Strategy for revenue diversification into investment or entrepreneurial options needs to be accompanied by significant attention to communication with all nonprofit audiences. This will absorb the most precious resources a nonprofit has—time. Consideration of the need for this intense education and communication process needs to be an explicit part of the decision to pursue revenue diversification in Strategy Area C. There will be no substitute for time invested in broad and deep communication to ensure institutional buy-in at all levels.

Business Planning Is Mandatory

Most nonprofits are not founded on real business plans, and most do not engage in business planning as a regular part of their operations. Nonprofits respond to a founder's mission and a perceived need for services on the societal commons. Mission and need drive programs. Detailed assessments of markets, competitors, relative value-propositions of alternative services or products, cost and revenue scenarios, and capital plans under alternative financing options are not usually the platform on which nonprofits are built. Nor are they the skills most nonprofit management programs teach, or the strengths of most nonprofit managers. But they are the fundamental skeleton on which revenue diversification in Strategy Area C must be built.

This prerequisite requires more than time, however. It requires skills, and therefore likely requires resources. A detailed business plan may be overseen by a board or advisory committee, but volunteers, however skilled, are unlikely to have the time to devote to developing the detailed plan. This means that outside consultants will need to be engaged, and those consultants will be expensive. This leads to the next strategy principle: Plan for costs.

Plan for Costs

Developing enterprise- or investment-based revenue strategies requires resources even before any firm decisions about strategy viability can be made. The early-stage costs of revenue diversification must be absorbed by a nonprofit's funds balance or by some offsetting philanthropic strategy, such as the acquisition of a planning grant, perhaps from that new entrepreneur board member with an entrepreneurial view of the future. The costs are likely to be significant, and so Strategy Area C is not for the faint of heart or for the nonprofit in financial crisis. Strategy Area C presumes that the nonprofit is relatively sophisticated, relatively stable, and focused on the relative long term. None of these characteristics describe a nonprofit in crisis; none are likely to exist in the vortex of a severe economic crisis.

Planning for diversification into enterprise or investment alternatives must be done in good times not in bad.

Link Everything Back to Engagement

As noted throughout this book, what sets nonprofits apart—what gives them their "nonprofitness"—is their role as mechanisms for engagement of people in problem solving in their communities, be that local, national, or global. If nonprofits are to hold true to that definition, revenue diversification in

Strategy Area C must not simply be about money. It must contribute to or empower engagement. The most financially successful and stable nonprofit that loses its link to community fails in its ultimate societal role.

Strategy Area C provides unique opportunities for revenue diversification to accomplish that goal. Alternative options bring the nonprofit in touch with whole new groups of leaders, whose loyalty can ultimately be extended from enterprise to philanthropy. New products and services provide new areas of interface with new publics. New approaches to service open up new opportunities to meet the needs of target clients.

This is what makes Strategy Area C exciting. True, it can provide revenue opportunities to build financial self-reliance. This, in turn, contributes to sustained, and even enhanced, service provision. But perhaps more important, it opens the nonprofit up to whole new audiences, whole new cohorts of leadership, which can become engaged not just in the revenue strategy, but in volunteerism, governance, and pure philanthropic support. The opportunity is to grow more diverse roots into community, which is the point of "nonprofitness" to begin with.

Pure Markets: Strategy Base = Linking to Outside Commercial Success

The final area of revenue diversification, Strategy Area D, takes the last and most constrained step. This step is to develop mechanisms to gain revenue not from the engagement of the nonprofit in markets themselves, but to link nonprofit revenue to the competitiveness of pure commercial organizations. The option clearly serves a fairly narrow audience of nonprofits because it assumes that the nonprofit owns or controls something that represents market value to commercial organizations. (See Exhibit 9.4.)

Successful strategies in Area D can be extremely useful for nonprofit efforts. The American Heart Association's licensing of its brand for healthy foods not only increases sales for companies awarded the right to use the brand, it also increases the market for healthy foods, itself a significant benefit to and by-product of the association itself. In addition, it throws off about $2 million in royalties revenue to the association for its programs, funds that are not tied to any particular use and so can be used at the discretion of the organization.

Project (RED) provides another robust example. The use of the (RED) brand by companies increases their sales, demonstrates their commitment to the Global Fund for HIV/AIDS, Tuberculosis, and Malaria, and has funneled millions of dollars to the fund for prevention and therapy programs in the developing world. The strategy is not premised on philanthropy. It is premised on consumer behavior. The hypothesis, now well-supported by

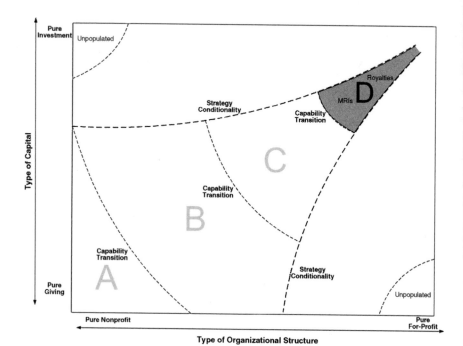

EXHIBIT 9.4 Strategy Area D: Markets

evidence, is that people will purchase the products of companies that are aligned with a compelling problem of the poor. And the companies will wish to reach those people because they can/will also buy other products of the company. A brand linked to commercial self-interest can throw off resources for societal needs even if the nonprofit itself does not engage in any commercial endeavor.

Similarly, mission-related investing can result in revenue to advance societal needs by moving capital to relevant commercial institutions. In turn, it throws off earnings to support the nonprofit purely from the commercial success of the unrelated commercial institution itself. Nothing philanthropic is actually taking place, but both nonprofit revenue and nonprofit mission are served.

There are three fundamental elements to strategy in Area D.

Take an All-of-Resources Approach

Revenue diversification in Strategy Area D requires that a nonprofit take an all-of-resources approach to its mission. An assessment must be made

The Evolution of Revenue Diversification

A Hypothetical Case of the Oak Street Soup Kitchen of Rivertown

Part IV: The Final Hurdle

FTK's new COO embarked on a market assessment and determined that FTK's products had achieved such local popularity, both for their origins in a social enterprise and for their quality recipe uniqueness, that market expansion was possible. He reprogrammed $150,000 in revenues and hired a management firm to develop a business plan to develop a partnership with a national food company, licensing the FTK brand and recipes for national production and distribution. The management consultants felt that $2 million in net revenues from royalties was not an unrealistic expectation. The plan also indicated that, to achieve its potential, FTK would need to move into larger operational quarters in a new industrial park 25 miles from its current and historical location in Rivertown's inner city.

Business plan in hand, the COO sent overtures to the five largest national food companies and ended up in a bidding war with Coast-to-Coast, its corporate supporter from the 1990s, and America Foods, which had just been purchased by investors from China. Neither company had operations in Rivertown.

The Kitchen hired its first general counsel to handle the looming process.

Community donations dropped to 5 percent of revenues. A delegation of elderly volunteers, most of whom had been ladling soup in the kitchen for at least a decade, made an appointment to see the executive director of the Kitchen. The meeting was set for a month later, the first available date on the director's calendar.

The volunteers brought unsettling news. Word in the community, both among volunteers and among the poor, was that the Kitchen no longer was committed to the needs of Rivertown and no longer valued, or even cared about, the community itself. It was getting nearly impossible to find new volunteers for the soup kitchen and food pantry, and the average age of the current volunteer force was 72. The volunteer delegation apologized to the executive director, but they needed to leave at precisely 10 A.M. to attend the funeral of a volunteer who had worked at the Kitchen for 25 years. Perhaps the executive director had not heard, but she had passed away suddenly last week, just after returning to her apartment from her work at the Kitchen. The delegation noticed that

(Continued)

> (*Continued*)
> there had not been any floral arrangement at the funeral home from the Kitchen.
>
> One week later, the Kitchen advertised for a director of fund development and community relations. Residence in Rivertown was a job requirement.

of all of its assets and all of its operations, and each of the pieces judged for its contribution to the intersection of mission and revenue. The first step is a complete, top-to-bottom, inside-out analysis of what resources or assets have potential commercial value consistent with mission. Because any opportunities identified are likely to be complex and require investment (see below), boards must be deeply involved and fully supportive of the effort.

Build Brand

In the world of commerce, brand is critical to success. An organization's brand is its promise. It represents what the consumer can always and everywhere expect from the company, and it underpins the relationship between company and consumer.

Most nonprofits do not take this approach to brand. A name is necessary for an organization, so a nonprofit has a name. The name may distinguish one nonprofit from another, or provide a certain image within the nonprofit sector, but a name is not usually seen in terms of a brand.

The nonprofit that wishes to assess options in Strategy Area D must determine whether and how its name can become a strong brand, the promise between itself and the societal commons that cements it to its clients, its board, its volunteers, and its community. This is complex work, with subtleties not well understood in the sector. Most nonprofit managers do not come from brand backgrounds, most boards do not think in these terms, and most nonprofit management training programs do not include brand assessment and strengthening skills in their curricula. Thinking in terms of brand, strengthening brand, and mobilizing brand to provide a value-proposition to commerce will require outside skills. And that will entail costs.

Acknowledge and Assess Costs

As in Strategy Area C, determining whether, and if so how, commercial linkages can be made or capital can be invested to contribute both to mission and to revenue stability takes a financial investment in outside expertise and in technical studies. Sophisticated market strategies will take money and time to develop, and money and time to implement. Again, the options cannot be developed in organizational crisis, nor in times of economic stress. Strategy Area D represents a playing field that nonprofits must assess over time and from positions of strength. There are no easy answers that shore up weakness in the near term.

Be Vigilant about Quality

Strategy Area D does not provide effortless and automatic revenue streams. Any available option requires constant and careful monitoring. Whether capital productivity or the use of brand, great damage can be done to an organization if linkages to commerce do not fill the sail of mission in ways that power the nonprofit on a productive course. The American Heart Association, for example, manages a vigilant technical committee to ensure that the licensing of its brand is only to heart-healthy products. Nonprofits who have tried similar strategies and not attended to quality have found themselves on the receiving end of media attention that seriously damaged their ability to serve their mission. In the end, the danger is that strategy intended to strengthen a nonprofit's service resources can destroy its community trust and its ability to achieve its core reason for being, engagement of people on the societal commons.

Vigilance requires time and resources, not to mention financial experts and lawyers. There are clear opportunities for growth in Strategy Area D, both in terms of revenues and in terms of the reach of a nonprofit relative to its programs and its mission. But the opportunities are accompanied by serious institutional risks. Only nonprofits with organizational depth and leadership strength can or should take those risks.

Crossing the Strategy Area Boundaries

As noted throughout this chapter, organizations that seek to diversify their revenue by moving among strategy areas face capacity transition barriers. These involve skills, organizational culture, management focus, and accountability expectations.

One key to developing strategy is to understand the progression that is needed within an organization to make movement possible. As with revenue strategies themselves, these are not exclusive characteristics. Capacities needed to be successful with expressive philanthropy strategies are not replaced but moving into evidence-based strategies. Rather, the capabilities are largely additive. With each progression, additional capacities are needed. Progression requires more and more capability and/or greater and greater diversity.

The Evolution of Revenue Diversification

A Hypothetical Case of the Oak Street Soup Kitchen of Rivertown

Part V: The Consequence: Was Mission the Price?

The story of the Kitchen is obviously apocryphal. However, it illustrates the degree to which the evolution of revenue diversification strategies require new approaches and new skills, so they require organizational change.

Revenue diversification can strengthen organizational finance and enable significant increases in the service capacity of a nonprofit. It can provide the financial stability that allows a nonprofit to weather economic hard times, storing up resources to steer through a storm of increased demand and declining revenues.

But there is a price. That price is a combination of two realities. First, more complex approaches to revenue require new skills and systems that are not always a natural extension of the types of human resources on which many nonprofits are built. Second, growth and evolution can lead a nonprofit toward a level of complexity that diverts its attention from its community base. The price of complexity can be losing closeness to the people. The latter effect may be totally unintentional, but the pressure of time and management can have consequences.

Exhibit 9.5 makes the point, tracing the capacity changes that are needed to the nonprofit's skill base, culture, management focus, and accountability focus as strategy areas are crossed.

The nonprofit that seeks to diversify its revenue into sources of support that expects clear evidence of impact does not replace its need for relationships. It adds onto those skills the quantitative skills needed to design programs capable of producing evidence and then analyzing and reporting on those results. Similarly, management does not need to replace its focus on raising money, but add to that focus an extra lens that demands that money actually leads to measurable impact. The organization does not excise its culture of charity, but must add to that the discipline of a culture focused on the actual performance of its efforts.

	Strategy Area A: Expressive Philanthropy	Strategy Area B: Rising Expectations	Strategy Area C: Quasi-Markets	Strategy Area D: Markets
Skill Base	Relationships with donors and volunteers	Evidence	Finance	Markets
Culture	Charity	Service performance	Financial performance	Brand performance
Management Focus	Money raised relative to needs	Impact on community	Institutional financial sustainability	Opportunistic flexibility in markets
Accountability Focus	Self and clients	Funders' priorities	Investors perceived ROI	Investors and markets

EXHIBIT 9.5   The Progression of Crossing the Capacity Barriers

The list goes on. The point is that revenue diversification, although critical to stability in economic hard times, does not come without a price. And the price is organizational complexity. Planning that complexity, and determining how much complexity is too much, is the subject of Chapter 10, "Prevent Where Possible, Cure Where Necessary."

Prevent Where Possible, Cure Where Necessary

Strategic Steps to Prepare for and Respond to Economic Crisis

I should esteem it the extreme of imprudence to ... expose the union to the jeopardy of ... the chimerical pursuit of a perfect plan. I never expect to see a perfect plan from an imperfect man.

Alexander Hamilton

Federalist Paper Number LXXXV

New York, August 15, 1788

The Chinese character for "crisis" is composed of two brush strokes, one meaning danger, the other meaning opportunity. Economic crisis conforms to that principle. As we have seen, preparing for and responding to economic crisis requires the ability to see the opportunity that comes with complexity, and the danger that is entailed in taking on more complexity than an organization's culture, structure, staff, management, and board can tolerate.

Thematic Summary

Panic is never a good thing. Anticipating the certainty of economic change is the first step to preventing its resulting erosion of revenue streams. Planning for that certainty helps to stem organizational crisis.

(Continued)

> (*Continued*)
> But no crystal ball is flawless; no plan is perfect. So it is critical to have in store a tool box that enables the nonprofit to react to the inevitable effects of economic downturn and cure the resulting injury as quickly as possible.

This is a delicate balance. It will almost never be a balance that is struck in panic. Therefore, every organization must understand what is critical to prevent organizational disequilibrium in the face of cyclic economic downturns. Still, it is also true that, as Alexander Hamilton has so wisely noted, all the best efforts to anticipate all eventualities will likely fail at some point. Therefore, every organization is best advised to also understand the key elements that are necessary to react should prevention fail.

Steps to Prevent Organizational Crisis in Economic Hard Times

Prevention is always better than cure, so let us begin with prevention. There are nine approaches to ensuring that economic crisis does not significantly disrupt the viability of a nonprofit organization.

Step 1: Expect Hard Times

Economic cycles are essential for economic health and development. They can be expected. They can be anticipated. If that is true, then they are not surprises. Consequently, plans can be drawn up to deal with them. If there is one lesson to be taken from the near panic of the nonprofit sector in 2008–2009, it is that contingency plans for economic downturns are essential. Prevention requires planning. No plan totally prevents organizational disruption. But plans can prevent panic.

Nonprofits should take careful stock of the lessons taught during the 2008–2009 period and assess what tactics were beneficial to their adjustment and what opportunities were missed. The learning must be committed to written record, executive directors, board members, and management staff change. Institutional memory may walk out the door before the next economic cycle. Return to these plans every two years; review them against current revenue structure and strategy. Update them so that they are not antiquated and useless when they are needed.

Step 2: Project the Future as a Base for Diversification Strategy

Purposeful diversification requires careful analysis of the operating environment of the future. Diversification takes time. Therefore the time frame that is important is not yesterday or today. It is tomorrow.

Diversification requires careful analysis of both programs and funding opportunities. Programs may need to be adjusted to take advantage of opportunities. Face that necessity and develop a reasonable, actionable strategy for making program changes. This means undertaking a comprehensive analysis and a 15-year projection of demographics and economics of target client populations and associated social and policy trends. Intersect this analysis with the revenue analysis to identify both opportunities and necessary changes. It is true that such an effort requires time, and that time is often the rarest of commodities for nonprofits. But there is no substitute for understanding where the world is going in determining where you should go.

Treat your mission like a sail, not an anchor. Plot a programs path to the future in alignment with the plot of a revenue diversification path to the future.

Step 3: Build a Strong Youth Base

With an aging population, organizational stability requires attention to building a robust engagement strategy focused on the young. To lead to lasting support, engagement must be more than token and grudging. It must provide meaningful and rewarding ways for young people to make a difference in their own terms. Strategy must be completely reviewed for relevance and for depth of engagement.

As noted in Chapter 4, "Emerging Nonprofit Revenue Parameters," the future will see not only an increasingly ethnically diverse youth population, but young people who look for and expect different ways of communicating and engaging. Strategy that looks to prevent organizational crisis in times of economic crisis must revamp youth engagement from organizational top to bottom, and from programs to volunteerism to funding to recognition. More of the same will not do. More of something different will be required.

Step 4: Place Revenue Diversity within a Business Model

The point of diversifying revenue is to develop a robust ability to adjust to economic challenge while still providing critical goods and services on the societal commons. But revenue diversification is a means not an end. Therefore, the end must be well understood. Revenue strategy must exist within a business model. The nonprofit's first internal analytic task is to reexamine its business model within the arc of change in its operating environment. Understanding the performance of the business model in that environment, and any necessary changes to the model, provides the structure within which revenue diversity takes place.

Valuing the Commitment of Young People in Philanthropic Strategy: Friends of Litewska Children's Hospital

The end of the Cold War meant not only the warming of political rela-tions between the former Soviet satellites and the West, but the opening up of society as well. With the fall of the Berlin Wall and the success of Solidarity, Poland quickly became a poster child for this process. In a manifestation of the old "teach a man to fish" adage, one of USAID's flagship health-care projects in the country was the establishment of the first-ever private philanthropic foundation to help renovate Litewska Children's Hospital in Warsaw, a project conceived and managed by my mother. Although I was only nine years old at the time, her vivid stories of patients carried up to surgery on doctors' backs when the elevators broke and of a hospital heated by manually fed coal furnaces had a major impact on me. Some friends and I had previously started a "club" to raise money for local hospitals during our summer vacations. Hearing the stories of how hard doctors had to work to provide the most basic care, we decided to dedicate our summer to lemonade sales for the hos-pital. I presented the fruits of our labor—a whopping $100—pinned to a teddy bear to the Friends of Litewska Children's Hospital Foundation in Warsaw.

As a wide-eyed elementary school student, the significance of the event was largely lost on me at the time. Only later, when my studies exposed me to ideas about civil society and the challenge posed by the post-Communist context, would I begin to see the importance of a private foundation finding roots in a society accustomed to decades of top-down management. The power of private philanthropy to enhance local capacity has become evident in the vast improvements in Litewska's record of care over the past decade. The nine-year-old with the $100 and a teddy bear thought she might be helping another nine-year-old. In retrospect, I see that she was part of a process with the potential to transform a society.

Jennifer Raymond
Ph.D. Candidate
Georgetown University

Without a clear understanding of the existing or future business model, revenue diversification risks willy-nilly wandering down multiple circuitous paths. All in the interest of hitting upon something that will lead somewhere. As Yogi Berra has famously observed, if you don't know where you are going, you might wind up somewhere else. Business model must precede revenue strategy.

Step 5: Diversify Revenue into at Least Strategy Area B

Begin to develop opportunities to diversify at least into Strategy Area B. Look for areas of alignment with venture capital, corporate, cause marketing, and institutional philanthropy. Deeply understand expectations. Pick those that are consonant with mission. Begin the cultivation process now. Do not wait for the next crisis.

Cultivation in Strategy Area B is as important as it is for expressive philanthropy. Diversification is not a matter of crafting proposals to be tossed over a funder's transom. Funders who have expectations for alignment with their own priorities or for clear impact must become as familiar and trusting of the soliciting nonprofit as any major donor. Indeed, because they have their own perspectives and desires, the need for trust can be even more compelling. However, trust will have to be created both at the level of the philanthropist or leader, and at the level of technical program staff. Cultivation will not just be a matter of personal relationships; it will also be a matter of peer relationships at the level of program. In Strategy Area B, the funder-nonprofit relationship is about mutual belief in mutual partnership for mutually perceived goals.

The process of diversification, therefore, will require deep research into possible alignments and proactive cultivation and engagement of both philanthropists and the program managers of institutional philanthropies. This will take time and effort. There is no short-cut.

Step 6: Inventory and Adjust Skills

Based on the assessments in Steps 3 and 4, take a careful and honest inventory of the internal staff and management skills of your nonprofit. Diversification, whether or not program adjustment is necessary, is likely to require new skill sets. This almost certainly will entail greater attention to and capacity for service outcomes and impact, and the social or economic dimensions of those impacts. This is not likely to be the end of the story, however.

Different skills or strategies for communications are also required. Nonprofits exist within community networks and cultures. Changing or diversifying approaches means communicating those changes to existing supporters and communities. Taking advantage of all media available—including electronic strategies—is increasingly an expected capacity.

Similarly, inventorying skills in management and at the level of the board should be done as a means to prepare for economic challenge as well as to diversify revenue. Critical characteristics that must be present in management and governance include deep experience with financial analysis and marketing/communications. To the extent that revenue diversification strategy entails taking on higher-risk commitments, such as program-related investments or diversification into social enterprise modes, these skills must receive extremely high priority if opportunities are to be actualized but closely managed and monitored.

Finally, depending on the outcomes of the operating environment analysis and projections, and decisions about program adjustment, the nonprofit skill base and that of the board need to be assessed relative to the likely service profile of the future. Is there greater need for linguistic or cultural diversity? Is there sufficient generational span on the board and in management? Does the volunteer pool reflect the future? Where will the future operating environment create leadership credibility problems for the nonprofit, and how might human resources pipelines be laid now in order to ensure that the progression to future leadership is smooth?

Step 7: Be Cautious about Government Funding

As has been noted in Chapter 3, "Philanthropy within Financial Structures," many nonprofits have taken on significant roles as the providers of services via government contracts and fee payments. The role of the nonprofit sector as a government partner is tremendously beneficial to the nation and to individual communities.

This growing dependency, however, creates vulnerability when economic crisis reaches its tentacles into public budgets, especially at the state and local level. Overdependence on government funds can lead to crippling problems when economies weaken because private funders are often loath to take on what can be perceived as government priorities. Two tactical elements are important in preparing for the nearly inevitable government funding effect of economic crisis.

First, from the beginning, blend private interests and leadership into publicly funded programs. Do not expect private funders to step into the breech if they have not been part of the effort from the beginning. Diversify funding within programs, as well as within the organizations.

Second, develop an "early-warning level" for government funding. The level will vary across organizations, but develop a conscious and explicit ratio threshold at which public monies are purposefully seen as representing an excessive role in program funding. This will provide a signal to begin strengthening the revenue diversity within the program, and the time to adjust.

Step 8: Look for Collaborative Opportunities Now

As noted in Chapter 8, "Common Principles for Robust Strategy," collaboration among nonprofits is often a difficult path to walk. Nevertheless, it is a path that many, many funders encourage, and even demand, in times of economic crisis. Constrained resources argue for demonstrations of efficiency and evidence that services and capacities are nonduplicative and value-producing.

Waiting until economic crisis hits and such funder expectations are on the table can leave nonprofits grasping for collaborative relationships. In turn, careful assessment and selectivity of affiliation can be sacrificed and the experience leave nonprofits less, rather than more, likely to join together to get programs efficiently to scale.

Coming out of the 2008–2009 recession, and with a long hill to climb back to robust economic growth, it is incumbent on nonprofits to search for collaborative opportunities. There is merit in that effort, not just in preparation for likely alliances to form at the next downturn, but because it is sensible to do so objectively. As noted in the introduction, the nonprofit sector has proliferated. There are myriad opportunities for nonprofits to join their programs together, squeeze out duplication, and together increase services and target real solutions to societal problems. Whether funders demand such collaboration in times of economic turmoil (and they will), the time for developing those relationships is now, when waters are calm and a way forward can be plotted, not when storms are blowing and the sea is in turmoil. Proactively seeking collaborations in normal times establishes a reputation for collaboration that draws resources toward you in times of crisis.

Map the relevant nonprofit sector. Identify and understand every nonprofit with either duplicative services (be honest about this), or services that are complementary or synergistic to your own. Have deep board discussion about program collaboration, about the advantages and risks of shedding the "we do it alone because we are best" view of the world for one that is more encompassing of other organizations. Do not wait for crisis and funder demands. Develop explicit criteria for collaboration. Make a top 10 list of organizations that fit programmatic goals or are synergistic with those goals. Develop deep knowledge about those organizations, their management, and their boards. Develop a strategy for collaboration with the leading three of the top 10.

Open up dialogue and discussions when times are good. The result could be better, more efficient service results. Almost certainly it will also be a reputation for innovation and collaboration that will attract philanthropy even in the hardest of economic times.

Step 9: Constantly Take the Pulse of Change

Almost nothing is true for very long anymore. Technological change is measured in heartbeats. Generational shifts are changing expectations and perspectives of societal problems and solutions. Ethnicity changes affect nearly every community. Wealth is to be found in new places and new cultures. It is insufficient simply to assess the 15-year arc of change, align it with business models and revenue, and then revert to business as usual.

Every nonprofit needs to be constantly taking the pulse of change in its operating environment. One of the obvious problems with innovation is that no single individual or organizational section is actually in charge of it. So there is never any clear accountability for tracking and adjusting to change. Unless responsibility for pulse-taking is clearly established and accountability for proffering the results to programs and management is clearly set, it will regularly fall to the bottom of everyone's "to do" list.

Establish a clear pulse-taking process and assign specific responsibility and specific reporting accountabilities. In turn, this also aids in anticipating the next economic cycle as the pulse-taking begins to detect early evidence of a skipped economic heart beat in the community.

Steps to Cure the Effects of Organizational Crisis in Economic Hard Times

Would that all problems could be prevented. They cannot. There is no perfect plan because we do not have perfect knowledge and perfect judgment. Therefore, it is likely that, however effective efforts to prevent organizational crisis, economic hard times will require organizational therapeutic action. Six general steps for moving from crisis to cure can aid the process.

Step 1: Move Quickly

The first trembles of the 2008–2009 deep recession actually began to be felt by mid-2007. By the end of January 2008, there was little doubt that hard times were coming. The market plummet of October 2008, then, was one of the final, not the first, indicators that the seas were roiling.

Too often, institutions (or all types, public and private) hope for the best. Hope is not a strategy. Keep one management eye on economic performance, and at the signs of trouble turn immediately to the prevention plan noted in Prevention Step 1 discussed earlier. Establish a system of incremental institutional steps to react and institute each step as needed. Adjust quickly and move incrementally.

Step 2: Engagement First, Last, and Always

Draw your supporters—of all types and financial sizes—toward you. A full 60 percent of those who stop supporting a nonprofit did so because they no longer felt involved with the organization.[1] Engagement of those who know of and support you is the best therapy to crisis. Reach out for their help, personal as well as financial. Turn to them for advice. Create new mechanisms, volunteer opportunities, or committees to bring them into the organization. Make them feel as though the fate of the organization is their fate as well because they are not just funders, they are peers and partners.

Get out of your office and go to the people. Do not expect or demand that they come to you. Meet with your supporters, your volunteers, your clients, your staff. Go to the people and engage them in conversation, in planning, in brainstorming. Give people a stake in the crisis, and that stake will preserve and strengthen loyalty.

Step 3: Engage and Expand the Board

For a corporation, board members have a minute-by-minute indicator of how things are going. Share price is their thermometer. It is difficult to miss organizational crisis when CNBC's commentators are broadcasting the pulse of hundreds of corporations every day and every hour.

The nonprofit sector does not have such mechanisms. Boards of directors are largely made up of volunteers. Few spend the majority of their time acting solely as nonprofit board members. Few have regular, public indicators of the health and well-being of the nonprofits on whose boards they sit. Therefore, board members may not be knowledgeable at an early stage that crisis is blooming.

The management temptation in crisis is to try to tamp down the problems short of board involvement. Many nonprofit managers see their boards as necessary, but not necessarily helpful in decision making. So nonprofits that manage a crisis as long as possible without board involvement can be seen as preferable to board "meddling" in decision making.

This is shortsighted. Early discussion of emerging problems and full development of alternative scenarios can embolden the board to reach out to its own networks to assist with solutions. Board understanding, involvement, and commitment are critical to cure.

Step 4: Communicate, Communicate, Communicate

When resources are under significant stress, there is a tendency to draw inward and to focus attention on adapting, coping, and at least surviving the economic crisis. Where budget slashing is needed, things that reach out are often sacrificed for things that reach inward to ensure staff stability, program provision, and central operations. This is understandable. It should also be the absolute last and final option, not the first.

Even more so than in good times, the nonprofit must communicate broadly and effectively with its multiple publics. The emphasis must not be just a plea in crisis. It must emphasize accomplishments and impacts. Communication must position solutions and value, not crisis and need. A critical step to cope with crisis is to push communications forward, not pull back.

Step 5: Look for Near-Term Collaboration

Whether or not a nonprofit has anticipated the opportunity for collaboration as noted in Prevention Step 8, in the midst of crisis the search for collaboration must be immediate with a primary emphasis on efficiency. Shared administrative services across nonprofits, shared information technology capacities, even shared technical capacities in such areas as evaluation and measurement need to be put in place quickly so that resources are leveraged.

This will require that management and boards be nimble, but it will also require that they be attentive to quality. Slap-dash solutions will lead to equal results. Again, the best mechanism to ensure that collaboration in crisis can be triggered quickly and with quality is to establish those relationships as part of a prevention strategy.

Step 6: Position for the Climb Out

No crisis lasts forever. It is true that economies hit hard times and never recover. The likes of ancient Rome and the Scythian Empire come to mind. But the U.S. economy is unlikely to ever resemble that history. Economic downturns are followed by recovery. True, the recovered economy seldom looks exactly like its past shadow. But recovery is the normal next economic cycle. And with recovery comes reengaged philanthropy.

Even as a nonprofit copes with crisis, an absolutely central step is to lay the groundwork for recovery and growth. This means putting in place at an early point an assessment and the organizational effects of the crisis, and a concrete development plan to ensure that the nonprofit is positioned, poised, indeed, perched, and ready to restore growth as the economy improves. Waiting to develop that plan until the economic corner is turned is waiting too long. The development plan must set out the sequence of recovery strategies and steps even as the crisis continues. It must be ready to climb out apace with the economy. Those who wait to plan will find themselves far behind those who are ready to act.

Final Comments: A Call to Leadership

Neither prevention nor cure will come with complacency. Both require insightful leadership. Both require time and skill. This—not economic crisis—is the real challenge for the nonprofit sector. The more complex economic cycles become—and they are likely to become ever more complex with globalization, instant communication, and technological advance—the more nonprofit leadership will need to anticipate, adjust to, and recover from economic change.

There is, therefore, a tremendous need in the sector for managers and leaders who are comfortable with change, who embrace flexibility, who in effect are excited about the prospects for mission to be a sail not an anchor. The most successful nonprofits in serving the societal commons will be those whose leaders, boards, and programs are (1) sufficiently courageous to focus on the horizon and (2) sufficiently disciplined to put in place navigational strategies that take advantage of the winds of change to build stable revenue strategies, anticipate upcoming storms, weather them when they blow, and move ever forward to better society.

Note

1. "Bank of America Study of High Net-Worth Philanthropy, 2008." Researched and written by the Center on Philanthropy at Indiana University.

CHAPTER 11

Reprise on Philanthropy
Why Bother?

I know the price of success: dedication, hard work, and an unremitting devotion to the things you want to see happen.
Frank Lloyd Wright

Clearly, there is no simple path to develop robust revenue strategies that will prepare for and weather economic hard times. Developing options, making choices, and preparing both people and systems for an increase in diversity in income streams requires time, attention, and concentration. For those who have time on their hands, this is not particularly discouraging. For most nonprofits, however, time, attention, and concentration are more than fully filled with the simple process of delivering the services inherent in mission.

Why bother, then? Certainly, the busy manager can posit, economies recover and, with recovery, traditional philanthropy flows. Certainly, with an adequate understanding of the mission's importance, that philanthropy comes without strings. Certainly, there is adequate growth in traditional sources of funding to sustain any reasonable plan for service and program growth. Why bother, indeed.

In part, the answer is that, as we have seen throughout Chapters 3 through 6, those assumptions are flawed. As philanthropy and philanthropic expectations change, funds will not necessarily flow simply because the mission and intentions of nonprofits are laudable. Conditions will be placed on those flows. Moreover, innovation is opening up entirely new types of flows in which resources are robust but the requisite organizational skills and sophistication are equally complex.

Nonprofits may have to bother because "bothering" is necessary for existence.

Beyond this new reality about the relationship between funders and nonprofits, however, rests a deeper reason to bother, a more fundamental rationale for exerting the effort necessary to ensure the evolution of the non-profit sector in ways that can accommodate a more effective and innovative role in addressing society's increasingly complex problems.

The role of the nonprofit sector is more than simply the delivery of goods and services. It is, as Chapter 2, "Setting the Larger Stage," has argued, also more than simply the transfer of cash from donors to deserving nonprofits. Neither the services nor the cash are immaterial, of course. Services help people, and cash pays the bills. But the true dif-ferentiator for a nonprofit is its ability to reflect the commitment of the people to a common good, and to provide a means whereby they can be engaged in that endeavor. Where problems are complex and/or new strate-gies provide new means for engagement, it is incumbent on a nonprofit to capitalize on innovation in the interests of maximum engagement and effectiveness.

Complex problems plus the obligations of the sector mean that openness to complex revenue streams is necessary. Charitable donations as a base of strategy are fundamental. But, where other dollars are available, other dollars should be put to work. Investments, cause marketing, volunteerism, venture philanthropy—all need to be viewed for their ability to contribute to mission. This is so not simply because those dollars pay the bills. It is also true because such new strategies reflect the creativity and innovation of people and institutions that wish to see the societal commons strengthened and innovate for that reason. The role of the nonprofit is to turn toward such innovation because it represents the commitment of people to the betterment of the commons, not to turn away from it because it represents complexity.

Thus, nonprofits need to adapt to and take advantage of complexity for two reasons. First, complexity empowers revenue diversity, and rev-enue diversity can help to ensure financial stability in economic hard times. Planning ahead and harnessing a nonprofit to diversify revenue strategies in good times is the best preparation for the challenges of economic bad times.

Second, new generations of philanthropists are examining the needs of the societal commons and developing new mechanisms for flowing funds to those needs. Empowering their commitment as leaders and the creativity of their innovations are part and parcel of the nonprofits' role as pathways for the engagement of people in the solution of their own problems. True, many of these new approaches may not fit old templates. True, some may not work. True, also, most require change and adaptation on the part of non-profits, in terms of management, skills, and systems. But innovation amidst complexity is always and everywhere opportunity.

And opportunity for betterment that is born of the engagement of the people on the societal commons is the business for which nonprofits were created.

CHAPTER 12

Making a Difference in the World by Aligning Yourself with the Poor

Michael P. Hoffman

G ood morning and welcome to the 2009 graduating class, future graduates, parents, grandparents, and other family members, President Drew
Bogner, vice president of development, Ed Thompson, alumni, faculty, staff,
my colleagues from Changing Our World, the board of trustees, friends,
officials, and Michael and Angela.

It is an honor to speak to you today. President Barak Obama is giving
the commencement address tomorrow at the second best Catholic college in
the country after Molloy, Notre Dame. One thing I can promise you is that,
in his speech, President Obama will not quote, as his main source, from the
New York Post, as I will. Nor will he predict the winner of the Preakness, the
second leg of horseracing's Triple Crown, which goes off tonight at 6:15 P.M.
I will predict the winner later in today's speech.

For the next 18 minutes, I am going to address myself directly to today's
graduates. In the 2008 annual report, your visionary president, Drew Bogner,
wrote that, over the last 50-plus years, Molloy has graduated more than
15,300 students who make a difference in the world. He also challenged
and encouraged all of us to be agents of transformation. Today, I will share
a little of my personal story. More important, I want to leave you with three
core principles that I believe can empower the class of 2009 to truly make a
difference in this beautiful and wonderful world. You leave Molloy today at
a time in our history like no other—with a world that is craving authentic,
global leadership. The title of my address is "Making a Difference in the
World by Aligning Yourself with the Poor." Anyone who knows me knows

---

This text is the commencement address as given by Michael P. Hoffman to the
graduating class of Malloy College at the Nassau Coliseum on May 16, 2009.

that I am not a person who is interested in theory. My goal is to give you some information you can actually use as you go out and make your way in the world.

There are three principles I want to talk about:

1. Always treat everyone the way you want to be treated.
2. Be reflective and read the official paper of record in the world, the *New York Post* every day, not online but hard copy if possible.
3. Be *authentic* and align yourself globally with the poor.

Before we begin, let me give you some context. To understand my remarks, you need to understand something about me. Most fundamentally, I believe that anything is possible. It is a hard belief to hold onto sometimes, but when I am tempted to question that fundamental view, I turn to the experiences of others.

At the time of the Twin Towers tragedy, we worked, pro bono, very closely with Mayor Giuliani and his wife, Judith, who was one of our employees. Changing Our World was asked to help manage the Twin Towers Fund, which raised and distributed more than $200 million for the families of police officers and firefighters who died on September 11, 2001. Mayor Giuliani said many times that Winston Churchill gave him the strength to get through September 11th and its aftermath.

Winston Churchill said: "We make a living by what we get; we make a life by what we give."

A sense of what is possible is also the hallmark of the best of American business. One of our clients is the Case Foundation, founded by Steve and Jean Case. Steve, of course, is the founder of AOL. Steve Case said: "Always trust your instincts."

So belief that anything is possible must be an important core platform for your lives. Crisis, tragedy, sheer personal stupidity can raise huge barriers to that belief.

Professor Nancy Koehn, who is in my opinion, one of, if not the most, passionate leaders I have ever met, teaches at the Harvard Business School and Omnicom University. Nancy wrote a case study on Abraham Lincoln and the Civil War that we studied this past summer. The case touched me in a very deep way and I wanted to share a piece of the case with you today as a way to begin to tell you about myself.

Nancy wrote: "Lincoln's private experience as president—what he felt, what motivated him, how he endured personal as well as public challenges—has not been widely studied or discussed.[1]

In mid-December, in the third year of the Civil War, Confederate forces had soundly defeated Union troops at Fredericksburg, Virginia. More than 13,000 federal soldiers had been killed, wounded, or were missing in a loss that many attributed to poor Union generalship. The president again became the focus of collective anger and frustration at the course of the war. 'If there is a worse place than Hell,' Lincoln said on hearing of the defeat at Fredericksburg, 'I am in it.'

In my life, there have been a few times when I have been in the reflective place that Lincoln describes here. I have hurt myself and others through sheer stupidity and lack of discipline. But these mistakes have all made me look deep inside myself and my soul so I could be humbled to the core of my being and learn from my mistakes and make the world a better place and actually fall deeply in love with God.

Ralph Waldo Emerson said something I love, which truly reflects the beautiful spirit of Molloy College: "The only true gift is a portion of yourself." So let me share a little about myself.

I know what it is to be a part of a family like yours and like the one you have formed among yourselves here at Molloy. I am one of five children from incredibly loving parents. My father, who died of colon cancer, was an elementary school teacher and then principal, actually my principal. His best friend was the janitor at the school. He told me many, many times while I was growing up to treat everyone the way you want to be treated. He would be very proud that I am talking today at a school that, among other great callings, is graduating future teachers. My soulful loving mother is also a school teacher.

I am married to a beautiful woman, Maggie, a registered nurse who is extremely proud that I am speaking at a great school that is graduating nurses. As Dorothy Day, the founder of the Catholic Worker, said to her biographer, "The greatest calling in this world is that of a nurse." I have three sensational children: Siobhan—13, Michael—11, and Shannon—7. I also own and breed thoroughbred race horses and wish I had a horse in the Preakness today, the second leg of the horseracing's Triple Crown. It is now time for my pick. My pick today for the Preakness is #5, Friesan Fire, and I have put a significant bet on this horse with all of the proceeds going to Molloy College. Prior to this speech, I don't believe Dr. Bogner included thoroughbred racehorses as agents of transformation. He might now.

So, I know the good of life. But I also know some things that are difficult.

I know what it is to serve. I went to West Point and did five years of service to our great country, including an assignment on a peacekeeping mission in the Sinai. While in the military, I learned the key to leadership is to always take care of your fellow team members first—in the military, the senior officer in charge always eats last.

I know what it is to search for meaning. After my service, I spent a year and a half in the Catholic Seminary reflecting and studying, trying to determine if I was called to be a Catholic priest. I was not—however, that time in the seminary changed my entire life. I wanted to totally dedicate my life to making the world a better place. While in the seminary, I worked in the public showers over the summer at the Holy Name Center for Homeless Men. This was in the heyday of the Bowery, when drugs and alcohol were very present. I lived on the corner of Bleecker and the Bowery—actually a great place for a 28-year-old crazy person like me to find himself. Father Ahern, one of my personal heroes, ran the shelter and Bill Shepherd was my supervisor at the public showers. Bill told me on day one that I had two jobs every day. To bring him coffee and, *most* important, treat every man who walked into the public showers with the respect and dignity they deserved—just as he or I would want to be treated. He also told me to never turn my back on anyone in the public showers, as they might kill me!

I know what it is to lose a job. After leaving the seminary, I went back to the homeless shelter for a year, and then worked with the Franciscan Sisters of the Poor in their international health-care ministry for 12 years. I would still be in that role if the Sisters had not sold their billion-dollar health-care system.

I know what it is to be overwhelmed by the enormity of what lies in front of you. I spent a lot of time at the Franciscan missions in the United States, Africa, Brazil, Italy, Poland, and Croatia. It was through the Sisters and their work in Africa that I came to deeply love the poor, and to believe that however huge the task seemed, there was a path to self-reliance and dignity for every human being.

And I know what it is to finally hit upon your life's calling. After losing my job with the Franciscans, I started my current company, Changing Our World, with one of my best friends of 22 years, Chris Watson, with a single goal: to take what I had learned in my life and change the world through the power of philanthropy. Now in our 10th year, we are fortunate enough to be part of the Omnicom Group, a Fortune 200, New York Stock Exchange Company, that acquired us four years ago. Today, we have more than 100 incredibly passionate employees globally, working with our wonderful, philanthropic clients and partners, all trying to make our world a better place through philanthropy.

Now let me turn to the first of the three principles I want to leave you with today.

I have learned that to be successful you have to treat everyone the way you want to be treated. It is the key to global understanding and world peace. The Tanenbaum Center for Interreligious Understanding has published a document that highlights the centrality of that golden rule in virtually every faith around the world. I will highlight just a few with direct quotes from the sacred texts which govern these religions.

Buddhism: "Hurt not others in ways you yourself would find hurtful."[2]
Christianity: "In everything do to others as you would have them do to you; for this is the law and the prophets."[3]

Confucianism: "Do not unto others what you do not want them to do to you."[4]

Hinduism: "This is the sum of duty; do naught unto others which would cause you pain if done to you."[5]

Islam: "Not one of you is a believer until he loves for his brother what he loves for himself."[6]

Judaism: "What is hateful to you, do not do to your neighbor: that is the whole of the Torah; all the rest of it is commentary."[7]

To our graduates today, I'm sure you already do live this universal value every day. You must use it as the basis for your personal leadership to make our world a better place and more peaceful place.

Now for the second principle around which you must orient your life. If you are not already doing so, read the official paper of record in the world every day. That paper is, of course, the *New York Post,* with the mandatory reading of the best gossip page in the world, Page 6, an excellent business section, and a very good sports section, especially for horseracing. This is not just my opinion. We worked with Senator Bradley on a project. Arguably, he is one of the most intelligent men in the world. It was very early in the morning and we were doing all of the morning TV broadcasts around the country. He yelled to me: "Mike do we have a paper out there?" I said, "Sir, we have the *Wall Street Journal,* the *New York Times,* and the *New York Post.*" Senator Bradley said: "Give me the *Post.*" Clearly, if *Newsday* had been one of the options, the Senator would have selected *Newsday.*

Perhaps unlike many of your habits, your parents will approve of adhering to this principle. On March 8th of this year, the *New York Post* announced, and I quote, "Despite Biz Cuts, Grads Getting Jobs" and went on to note that "the brighter than expected jobs report is welcome news to students and placement officers alike," and I would add your parents.

Treating others as you want to be treated and becoming a daily reader of the *New York Post* prepares you for the last, most complex principle: Align yourself with the poor.

Again we turn, where else, to the *Post,* which pointed out on March 9th that however much the rest of us face this recession with fear, the world's poor bear the brunt of the crisis. World Bank President Robert Zoellnick remarked in that article that "we need to react in real time to a growing crisis that is hurting people in developing countries" and that action is needed by everyone including governments and multilateral institutions "to avoid social and political unrest."

Action. But what action?

My personal commitment to philanthropy is to change the world. So, is "action" money? Yes, money is important—you do not feed people, vaccinate babies, educate children, create jobs and prosperity with good wishes. But aligning with the poor means more than money.

I believe aligning with the poor means supporting them and empowering them not just in their poverty, but with the real means to aid their progress. We all, every one of us, wants to create a better life. We all strive to become more than we are now. Therefore, I use the words "align with the poor" intentionally. By aligning ourselves with the poor, we see their progress as essential to our own. This is not a matter of giving a dollar and walking away feeling better about yourself. It is about identifying with the poor and being satisfied with nothing less than their betterment, because nothing less is acceptable to us in our own lives.

Now that we have established and confirmed our hypothesis that to be successful in your careers and be global leaders, you have to treat everyone the way you want to be treated. And now that you will be reflecting on and reading the *New York Post* on a daily basis as well as carrying it around so people underestimate you every day (I love it when people underestimate me) we have learned we must align ourselves with the poor as partners. Let me now give you five real-world examples of leaders who believe that in order to be successful you must understand and care deeply about the poor.

The first one is Katherine Nesbeda, who joined Changing Our World right after her graduation from NYU. Katherine is a beautiful, incredibly smart, very spiritual, and religious woman who wanted to work at Changing Our World on international accounts to make a difference in the world. Many times, she gave me great spiritual advice to keep me close to God. After four years, she told me she had to leave Changing Our World because God had called her to work among the poor, with Doctors Without Borders, in one of the most dangerous places in the world, the Congo.

The second is Frederic de Narp, the President and CEO of Cartier North America, the number one luxury brand in the world of the rich and famous. Frederic is a great friend of mine.

At one point in his career, Frederic left Cartier and went to work in Haiti with his wife to understand and serve the poor and then returned to Cartier as he felt he could do more to help the poor as a global leader. At Cartier, he created the LOVE program, which aligns Cartier's Love collection with celebrities and their charities around the world. As of today, the LOVE Program has given close to $4 million to charities. Frederic has told me on many occasions to understand the rich, you must be authentic and be equally as comfortable and respectful with the poor.

The third example is Pattie Sellers, editor at large at *Fortune* and arguably one of the most influential women in the world. She would die if she heard me say that but I believe it to be true. Pattie wrote the *Fortune* cover story about Melinda Gates, titled "The $100 Billion Woman."

Pattie chairs the annual FORTUNE Most Powerful Women Summit (the top women leaders in business, philanthropy, government, academia, and the arts) and has started the *Fortune*/U.S. State Department Mentoring Program, which partners young women leaders from around the world with the top American women leaders, including Fortune 500 CEOs. Pattie knows that to make our world a better place, you must align yourself and understand and partner with the future leaders in our world.

My fourth example returns us to Haiti. Susie Krabacher, a former Playboy centerfold who lived a self-described wild life, has given her life to the poor in Haiti. Many of the wealthiest and most influential leaders right here in Long Island have aligned themselves with Susie because they believe in her and, like her, believe you must align yourself with the poor.

Susie and her husband, Joe, started Mercy & Sharing in 1995 after Susie went on a trip to Haiti with a friend from her church. Mercy & Sharing is not a means of providing charity but is a means of providing opportunity to thousands of abandoned and orphaned children in Haiti. For 14 years, they have tirelessly given their own money and raised funds and awareness for Mercy & Sharing's orphanages, schools, medical clinic, and feeding programs in the poorest country in the Western Hemisphere, often themselves spending two of every eight weeks in Haiti.

My final example is a project that proves that every one of us, no matter how young or how old, no matter whether we graduated 40 years ago or 40 minutes ago, every one of us can find a practical, immediate, and meaningful way to align with the poor.

This past January in Davos, Switzerland, Bill and Melinda Gates invited all of us in this room to partner with them to wipe out Neglected Tropical Diseases around the world—in Africa, Latin America, and Asia. Even though my company works for the Bill and Melinda Gates Foundation and the Global Network for Neglected Tropical Diseases, I was fortunate enough to be at the announcement with Bill and Melinda Gates as a donor, through the Hoffman Fund established in honor of my father from Hillburn, New York.

Melinda Gates, who is just an unbelievable passionate leader, said in Davos: "For governments, corporations, NGOs, and individuals, there is little else during this global economic crisis that provides such a significant return on investment while also reducing suffering and saving lives."

Bill Gates said, "Our work together to help the world's poor is more important in the face of this global financial crisis."

At Davos, "... the Global Network for Neglected Tropical Diseases announced that it had received $34 million through a grant from the Bill and Melinda Gates Foundation to step up the global effort to prevent and treat neglected tropical diseases that affect 1.4 billion people worldwide who live on less than $1.25 per day. For approximately 50 cents per person per year, the seven most common neglected tropical diseases can be effectively treated ... I would encourage everyone to look at (www.just50cents.org) that educates users about the impact NTDs can have on children and communities and illustrates the incredible difference that even a 50 cent donation can make ..." Kari Stoever, Managing Director of the Global Network, another incredibly passionate and brilliant leader said, "We are guided by the principle: Never underestimate what you can do when you know what can be done."

How great it is that the wealthiest people in the world have provided a way for all of us in this arena to partner with them in aligning ourselves with the poor. Bill and Melinda Gates have invited all of us to be their partners in wiping out neglected tropical diseases in the world. For just 50 cents, you can partner with Bill and Melinda Gates and save a life. How incredible is that? For the same cost as a *New York Post,* you can save a life.

Now that you are graduates, please remember that for the rest of your lives you will represent Molloy College. Your achievements, the diploma in your hand today, bestows on you the honor of that role. For the rest of your lives, you represent not just your families but the larger family of Molloy itself. Live true to President Bogner's words. Make a difference in the world. Make a difference by always keeping at the center of your lives three principles:

1. Always treat everyone the way you want to be treated.
2. Be reflective and read the official paper of record in the world, the *New York Post* every day, hard copy if possible.
3. Be *authentic* and align yourself globally with the poor.

God bless all of you and God bless our beautiful world that is crying out for all of the Molloy College graduates today to join the other 15,300 Molloy graduates and make a significant impact in making a difference in the world and making our world a more beautiful and peaceful place.

Thank you for the honor and privilege of speaking to you today. And congratulations to you all.

Notes

1. "Letter to James C. Conkling," excerpted from *Lincoln, The Collected Works,* vol. 6.
2. Udana-Varga, 5:18.
3. Matthew, 7:12.

4. *Analects*, 15.13.
5. The *Mahabharata*, 5:1517.
6. Fortieth Hadith of an-Nawawi, 13.
7. Talmud, *Shabbat*, 31a.

Index